Flavors *of* Fall

CENTENNIAL KITCHEN®

CENTENNIAL BOOKS

Flavors *of* Fall

CENTENNIAL KITCHEN®

Pumpkin Bread Pudding
With Honey-Bourbon
Whipped Cream, page 112

Table of Contents

Croissant
Breakfast
Casserole,
page 8

quick tip

For the best texture,
toast buttery croissants
before mixing with other
casserole ingredients.

chapter one

Breakfasts & Brunch

Rise and shine with these hearty ways to start the day, from cheesy casseroles to French toast stuffed with bacon and cream cheese.

Croissant Breakfast Casserole

Using croissants instead of bread makes this an extra-indulgent way to start the day.

FAMILY FAVORITE | SPECIAL OCCASION
TIME 1 hour, 45 minutes
(15 minutes active)
MAKES 10 to 12 servings

INGREDIENTS

Cooking spray
1 tablespoon canola oil
1 pound breakfast sausage meat
1 bunch scallions, sliced
1 small sweet potato, peeled and grated
2 cups chopped spinach
2 teaspoons fresh sage, minced
8 large eggs
3 cups whole milk
1 cup heavy cream
1¼ teaspoons kosher salt
1 teaspoon ground black pepper
2 cups shredded white cheddar cheese, divided
6 croissants, cubed and toasted for 5 minutes

1. Preheat oven to 350 F. Coat a 2½-quart dish with cooking spray.
2. In a large skillet over medium-high heat, warm oil. Add sausage and brown, breaking up with a spoon, about 5 minutes. Add scallions (reserving some for garnish), sweet potato, spinach and sage, stirring to combine. Cook for 1 to 2 minutes more until spinach is slightly wilted. Remove from heat and set aside to cool for 10 minutes.
3. In a large mixing bowl, whisk together eggs, milk, cream, salt and pepper. Stir in 1 cup cheese. Add croissants, tossing to combine. Stir in cooled sausage mixture. Pour into baking dish; let rest at room temperature for 20 to 30 minutes to allow croissants to soak up custard. (If you have time, cover with plastic wrap and refrigerate overnight.) Top with remaining cheese.
4. Bake for 40 to 50 minutes or until golden brown and center is firm. Garnish with remaining scallions.

Cinnamon-Sugar Apple Cider Muffins

These are a cinch to prepare!

EASY | VEGETARIAN
TIME 30 minutes
(10 minutes active)
MAKES 12 muffins

INGREDIENTS

Cooking spray
2 cups all-purpose flour
¾ cup sugar
2 teaspoons baking powder
½ teaspoon kosher salt
1 teaspoon cinnamon
2 eggs, beaten
2 tablespoons vegetable oil
½ cup apple cider or juice
¼ cup milk

FOR THE TOPPING

½ cup sugar
1 tablespoon cinnamon
¼ cup butter, melted

1. Preheat oven to 350 F. Line a muffin tin with paper liners and lightly coat with cooking spray.
2. In a mixing bowl, whisk together flour, sugar, baking powder, salt and cinnamon. In a separate bowl, whisk together eggs, oil, cider and milk. Stir egg mixture into flour mixture and spoon into prepared muffin cups.
3. Bake for 15 to 20 minutes or until a tester comes out clean. Set aside to cool slightly.
4. To make topping: In a small bowl, whisk together sugar and cinnamon. Brush tops with melted butter and dip each into the cinnamon-sugar mixture.

Cream Cheese & Bacon–Stuffed French Toast

This is a great use for any day-old bread you have, which absorbs the custard better.

EASY | FAMILY FAVORITE | QUICK
TIME 20 minutes (all active)
MAKES 8 servings

INGREDIENTS

16 slices (about ¾ to 1 inch thick) day-old soft white bread
1 cup cream cheese, softened, divided
8-10 bacon strips, cooked and cooled
2 tablespoons confectioners' sugar, plus more for garnish
½ cup whole milk
6 eggs
1 teaspoon vanilla extract
1 teaspoon cinnamon
¼ teaspoon nutmeg
Pinch of salt
½ cup butter, divided
Maple syrup, for serving

1. On 8 slices of bread, spread 2 tablespoons cream cheese. Cut bacon strips into thirds and arrange on top of cream cheese; top each with remaining slice of bread, as if making a sandwich.
2. In a wide, shallow baking dish, whisk together sugar, milk, eggs, vanilla, cinnamon, nutmeg and salt. Dip each sandwich in custard mix, turning to coat completely.
3. In a skillet over medium heat, warm butter, 1 tablespoon at a time, and fry each sandwich, 2 to 3 minutes per side or until golden brown. Garnish with a dusting of confectioners' sugar and serve with maple syrup.

**Cream Cheese &
Bacon–Stuffed
French Toast**

Overnight Slow-Cooker Apple Butter

Let the slow cooker work while you sleep—then wake up to fresh-made apple butter, ready to spread on toast or waffles.

EASY | MAKE-AHEAD | VEGETARIAN
TIME 12 hours (30 minutes active)
MAKES 4 pints

INGREDIENTS

- 6-7 pounds apples, peeled, cored and chopped
- 1 cup sugar
- ¾ cup light brown sugar, packed
- ¼ cup unsulphured molasses
- ¼ teaspoon ground cloves
- ½ teaspoon kosher salt
- 2 cinnamon sticks

1. Place all ingredients in slow cooker; stir to combine. Set slow cooker to low and cook for 10 hours or until mixture is thickened and dark brown. Remove cinnamon sticks and discard.

2. Use an immersion blender to blend the apple mixture until smooth. Cook, uncovered, for 2 hours, stirring occasionally.

3. Spoon apple butter into airtight containers and refrigerate for up to a week.

No-Bake Pecan Date Bites

If your dates seem a little dry, try adding more honey to the mixture to make these chewy treats.

EASY | QUICK | VEGETARIAN
TIME 10 minutes (all active)
MAKES 16 to 20 servings

INGREDIENTS

- 2 cups pecans
- 18 Medjool dates
- 2 tablespoons honey
- ½ teaspoon cinnamon
- ½ teaspoon kosher salt
- Cooking spray
- 1 cup toasted coconut

1. Place all of the ingredients except coconut in the bowl of a food processor. Pulse until the mixture comes together.

2. Spray hands lightly with cooking spray and roll mixture into bite-size balls.

3. In a wide, shallow dish, add coconut; roll date balls in coconut to coat.

4. Let the bites chill in the refrigerator or freezer for about an hour before enjoying. The bites can be stored in the refrigerator for up to 2 weeks or in the freezer for up to 3 months.

Fall Root-Vegetable Hash

This recipe is a great way to use up any vegetables in your fridge that seem like they are about to lose their freshness.

EASY | QUICK | VEGETARIAN
TIME 25 minutes (all active)
MAKES 4 servings

INGREDIENTS

- ¼ cup unsalted butter, divided
- 1 leek, trimmed, halved lengthwise, cut crosswise into ¼-inch slices
- 1 rib celery, thinly sliced
- 2 carrots, peeled and diced
- 1 parsnip, peeled and diced
- 1 small white turnip, diced
- 1 medium Yukon Gold potato, diced
- ¼ cup vegetable broth
- ½ teaspoon kosher salt
- ¼ teaspoon ground black pepper
- 4 large eggs

1. In a large skillet over medium-high heat, melt half of butter. Add leek and celery; saute until softened (about 5 minutes); add remaining ingredients

No-Bake Pecan Date Bites

(except eggs). Cook, stirring often, until vegetables are soft (about 10 to 12 minutes).

2. In a large nonstick skillet over medium-high heat, melt remaining butter. Fry the eggs until desired doneness. Divide vegetable mixture among 4 serving plates and top with egg.

Oat-Cranberry-Bacon Breakfast Cookies

Make extra bacon with breakfast on Saturday, then bake these salty-sweet cookies with the leftovers on Sunday.

EASY | FAMILY FAVORITE | QUICK
TIME 30 minutes
(12 minutes active)
MAKES 1 dozen cookies

INGREDIENTS

- ½ cup butter
- ½ cup sugar
- ¼ cup light brown sugar
- 1 egg
- 1 cup all-purpose flour
- ¼ teaspoon baking soda
- 6 strips bacon, cooked and crumbled
- 1 cup oats
- 1 cup wheat flake breakfast cereal (such as Wheaties)
- ½ cup dried cranberries

1. Preheat oven to 350 F. Line 2 baking sheets with parchment paper.
2. In a stand mixer with a paddle attachment, or using a hand mixer, cream butter and sugars until fluffy. Beat in egg. In a medium bowl, whisk together flour and baking soda; gradually beat into butter mixture. Stir in bacon, oats, cereal and cranberries.
3. Drop rounded tablespoons onto baking sheets, leaving 2 inches

Breakfast Rice Bowl With Avocado & Edamame

of space between each cookie.
4. Bake for 15 to 18 minutes. Let cool on a wire rack.

Breakfast Rice Bowl With Avocado & Edamame

Thanks to two microwave-friendly products, this vegetarian breakfast comes together in just a few short minutes.

EASY | QUICK | VEGETARIAN
TIME 10 minutes (all active)
MAKES 2 servings

INGREDIENTS

- 1 (8.5-ounce) package microwavable jasmine rice (such as Ben's Original)
- 1 small shallot, diced
- ¼ cup pistachios, chopped
- 1 cup frozen edamame
- 1 avocado, peeled and sliced
- 1 tablespoon unsalted butter
- 2 eggs
  Pinch of kosher salt
  Pinch of ground black pepper
  Hot sauce, for finishing

1. Prepare rice according to package directions. Place in a large bowl and stir together with shallot and pistachios. Divide between 2 serving bowls.
2. Prepare edamame according to package directions. Divide edamame and avocado between serving bowls.
3. In a nonstick skillet over medium-high heat, melt butter. Add eggs, sprinkle with salt and pepper, and fry until desired doneness. Top each bowl with egg; sprinkle with hot sauce to taste.

Chocolate-Banana Muffins

These treats have it all—chocolate, oats and a hint of cinnamon

EASY | FAMILY FAVORITE | VEGETARIAN

TIME 35 minutes
(10 minutes active)

MAKES 12 muffins

INGREDIENTS

- Cooking spray
- ½ cup sour cream
- 1 teaspoon vanilla extract
- 1 large egg
- ¼ cup butter, melted
- 2 large ripe bananas, peeled and mashed
- ¾ cup sugar
- 1 cup old-fashioned oats
- 1½ cups all-purpose flour
- ½ teaspoon cinnamon
- 2 teaspoons baking powder
- ½ teaspoon baking soda
- ½ teaspoon salt
- ½ cup semi-sweet chocolate morsels

FOR THE TOPPING

- ¼ cup light brown sugar
- ¼ cup old-fashioned rolled oats
- 2 tablespoons all-purpose flour
- ¼ teaspoon cinnamon
- ¼ cup unsalted butter, at room temperature

1. Preheat oven to 350 F. Line a muffin tin with paper liners and lightly coat with cooking spray.
2. In a mixing bowl, whisk sour cream, vanilla, egg, butter, bananas and sugar. In a separate bowl, stir oats, flour, cinnamon, baking powder, baking soda and salt. Add chocolate and toss to coat.
3. Stir banana mixture into flour mixture. Spoon batter into muffin cups.
4. In a small bowl, mix topping ingredients with your hands. Sprinkle over muffins. Bake 20 to 22 minutes.

Potato, Fennel, Spinach & Feta Frittata

quick tip

Keep your cast-iron well seasoned: Dry thoroughly after rinsing with hot water (no soap) and lightly wipe with neutral oil.

Potato, Fennel, Spinach & Feta Frittata

Unlike scrambled or fried eggs, frittatas can be served at room temperature, so late sleepers don't have to miss out if they aren't up in time.

SPECIAL OCCASION | VEGETARIAN

TIME 40 minutes
(20 minutes active)

MAKES 8 servings

INGREDIENTS

- ¼ cup unsalted butter
- 2 small Yukon Gold potatoes, cubed
- ½ small fennel bulb, plus fronds for garnish
- 1 garlic clove, minced
- 3 cups baby spinach leaves
- 1 cup feta cheese, cubed
- 8 eggs
- ¼ cup half-and-half
- ½ teaspoon kosher salt
- ½ teaspoon ground black pepper
- ¾ teaspoon baking powder

1. Preheat oven to 400 F.
2. In an 8- to 10-inch oven-safe or cast-iron skillet, warm butter over medium heat. Add potatoes and saute until potatoes are beginning to soften and brown, stirring often, about 10 minutes. Add fennel and saute until softened, about 5 minutes.
3. Reduce heat to medium-low; add garlic and spinach, and stir to wilt slightly, about 2 minutes. Stir in cheese.
4. In a large mixing bowl, whisk together remaining ingredients. Pour into skillet and tilt the pan to make sure vegetable mixture is completely covered. Place skillet in oven and bake until frittata is puffed and golden, about 15 minutes.

5. Let cool slightly in the skillet before slicing. Run a knife around the edge of the frittata to loosen it from the skillet. Garnish with fennel fronds before serving.

5 Favorite Frittata Combos

Using the base recipe of 8 eggs, ¼ cup half-and-half, ½ teaspoon each salt and pepper, and ¾ teaspoon baking powder, add any of these tasty combinations:

❶ BROCCOLI & CHEESE 2 cups broccoli florets sauteed with 1 minced garlic clove; 3 ounces diced smoked ham; 1 cup shredded cheddar cheese

❷ MARGARITA PIZZA 3 cups baby spinach leaves; 2 cups grape tomatoes; 1 cup baby mozzarella balls; 1 teaspoon lemon zest

❸ LOX-STYLE 3 ounces chopped smoked salmon; 3 chopped scallions; 2 tablespoons drained capers; 2 tablespoons minced dill; 4 ounces crumbled goat cheese

❹ SPANISH 2 small potatoes, cubed and sauteed with 1 chopped and seeded red bell pepper and 1 minced garlic clove; ½ cup diced salami; ½ cup shredded manchego cheese

❺ ITALIAN 2 links Italian sausage, cooked and crumbled; ½ small fennel bulb, chopped and sauteed with 1 cup broccolini and 1 minced garlic clove; ¼ cup grated Parmesan cheese

Sausage &
Cheese
Biscuits

quick tip

Use your sharpest knife
to cut the biscuit dough;
clean edges help them
rise when baking.

Pumpkin Spice Latte Smoothie

Sausage & Cheese Biscuits

Cut and freeze these all-in-one breakfast biscuits ahead of time; they can go straight from the freezer to the oven.

―――――――

FAMILY FAVORITE | MAKE-AHEAD
TIME 40 minutes
(15 minutes active)
MAKES 12 to 16 biscuits

INGREDIENTS

- 3 cups self-rising flour, plus more for dusting
- ½ cup unsalted butter, diced
- 1 cup grated sharp cheddar cheese
- 2 scallions, sliced
- 1 pound breakfast sausage meat
- 1 cup buttermilk

1. Preheat oven to 425 F.
2. In a mixing bowl, add flour. Add butter; use hands or a pastry cutter to evenly distribute butter so mixture is crumbly.
3. In separate bowl, toss cheese and scallions lightly in a small amount of flour; add to mixing bowl, then toss in sausage and buttermilk. Mix with hands to combine.
4. Transfer dough to a lightly floured parchment sheet and pat or roll into an 8x10-inch rectangle,

¾- to 1-inch thick. Cut dough evenly into 12 to 16 squares.
5. Transfer parchment to a baking sheet and bake for 20 to 25 minutes or until golden brown. Break apart to serve.

Pumpkin Spice Latte Smoothie

Canned pureed pumpkin is an easy—and healthy—addition to almost any smoothie.

―――――――

EASY | QUICK | VEGETARIAN
TIME 5 minutes (all active)
MAKES 1 serving

INGREDIENTS

- ¾ cup brewed chilled coffee
- 1 tablespoon honey
- ½ cup canned pumpkin pie filling
- ½ cup vanilla yogurt
- ¼ peeled and sliced banana
- ½ cup ice cubes
  Pinch of nutmeg
  Pinch of cinnamon, plus more for garnish
  Pumpkin seeds (pepitas) for garnish

Place all ingredients in the blender jar, beginning with liquids. Blend on low speed for 5 to 7 seconds, stopping to scrape down the sides of the jar with a spatula if needed. Blend on high speed for 3 to 5 seconds to fully mix. Serve immediately; garnish with a dusting of cinnamon and some pumpkin seeds.

5 Fall-Flavor Smoothie Combos

Using the same recipe instructions as above, try any of these cool-weather combinations.

―――――――

❶ SALTED CARAMEL
¾ cup strong brewed chilled coffee; ½ cup 2% Greek yogurt; ¼ peeled and sliced banana; 2 tablespoons caramel sauce; pinch of sea salt
❷ PECAN PIE ½ cup 2% milk; ¾ cup vanilla yogurt; 1 tablespoon molasses, 2 chopped pitted dates; 2 tablespoons pecan butter; ½ peeled and sliced banana
❸ CINNAMON-APPLE
½ cup 2% milk; ½ cup vanilla yogurt; 1 teaspoon honey; ½ cup old-fashioned oats; 1 small cored, peeled and chopped apple; pinch of cinnamon
❹ S'MORES ¾ cup 2% milk; ½ cup vanilla yogurt; 2 tablespoon marshmallow cream; ½ peeled and sliced banana; 2 crumbled graham crackers; 1 tablespoon cocoa powder
❺ MEXICAN HOT CHOCOLATE ¾ cup low-fat chocolate milk, ½ peeled and sliced banana; splash of vanilla extract; squeeze of lime juice; 2 teaspoons cocoa powder; ½ teaspoon dark chili powder; pinch of cinnamon; ½ cup ice

Start With a Slice of Toast...

Then go way beyond plain old peanut butter and set out a different kind of breakfast spread with these flavorful combinations for busy mornings. Creamy avocado and smoked salmon, hummus and tangy tomatoes, mashed eggs and briny pickles.... The possibilities are only limited by your imagination.

❶ GOAT CHEESE & PISTACHIO Spread with 2 tablespoons goat cheese. Top with 1 tablespoon pistachios; drizzle with honey.

❷ ALMOND BUTTER & BANANA Spread with 2 tablespoons almond butter. Top with 1 sliced banana and 1 tablespoon finely grated carrot.

❸ AVOCADO & SALMON Spread with half an avocado, smashed. Top with ½ ounce chopped smoked salmon, a sliced radish and chopped dill.

❹ HUMMUS & TOMATO Spread with 2 tablespoons hummus. Top with ¼ cup halved grape tomatoes and 1 tablespoon toasted pine nuts. Garnish with fresh chopped parsley.

❺ EGG & PICKLES Spread with 2 hard-boiled eggs mashed and stirred together with 1 tablespoon mayonnaise. Top with 1 tablespoon chopped pickles; drizzle with hot sauce.

Cheesy Hash Brown Cups With Baked Eggs

This recipe is easy to double if you need to feed a crowd.

EASY | FAMILY FAVORITE | VEGETARIAN

TIME 40 minutes
(10 minutes active)

MAKES 6 servings

INGREDIENTS

Cooking spray

10 ounces refrigerated hash browns (such as Simply Potatoes)

2 tablespoons unsalted butter, melted

½ cup shredded cheddar cheese, divided

6 eggs

¼ teaspoon kosher salt

Chopped fresh parsley, for garnish

Red pepper flakes, for garnish

1. Preheat oven to 400 F. Coat a 6-hole muffin tin with cooking spray; set aside.

2. Place hash browns on paper towels and blot or squeeze to remove as much moisture as you can. In a medium bowl, toss hash browns with melted butter.

3. Divide hash browns evenly among muffin cups, firmly pressing the mixture into bottoms and up the sides. Spray filled cups with cooking spray and bake for 20-minutes or until edges are beginning to brown and crisp up.

4. Remove tin from oven, sprinkle 1 tablespoon cheese on each cup, then top each with an egg and a pinch of salt. Return to oven and bake for 8 minutes more or until egg whites are set. Garnish with parsley and pepper flakes.

quick tip
Use medium eggs for these hash brown cups. They'll fill the cup without spilling over.

quick tip

Be sure to use baking powder, not baking soda (which has a strong alkaline flavor), for crispy oven-baked wings.

Chipotle-Maple
Chicken Wings,
page 21

chapter two

Party Starters & Cocktails

Whether you're headed to a tailgate or gathering at home, these appetizers and drinks are sure to please any crowd.

Start With a Block of Cream Cheese...

Then simply stir in flavorful additions for a quick and easy party dip or spread. Just add crackers or crudités.

① PUMPKIN-PECAN
In a food processor, pulse softened cream cheese, ¾ cup canned pumpkin puree, ¼ cup chopped toasted pecans, 1 tablespoon honey and a pinch of kosher salt.

② SMOKED SALMON
Finely chop 2 ounces of smoked salmon and stir into softened cream cheese, along with 2 finely chopped scallions, ¼ teaspoon kosher salt, ¼ teaspoon ground black pepper and a squeeze of fresh lemon juice.

③ FALL GREENS
Thaw 1 cup frozen chopped spinach or collard greens, and squeeze between paper towels to remove water. Stir into softened cream cheese along with ½ finely chopped green bell pepper, ½ teaspoon kosher salt and ½ teaspoon ground black pepper.

④ ROASTED RED PEPPER
In a food processor, pulse softened cream cheese, 2 jarred roasted red peppers, ½ teaspoon smoked or sweet paprika, ¼ teaspoon kosher salt and a pinch of cayenne pepper.

⑤ LEMON-PEPPER
Zest one lemon and stir into softened cream cheese, along with half the lemon's juice and 1 teaspoon ground black pepper.

Chipotle-Maple Chicken Wings

Sure, you could fry 3 pounds of chicken wings, but why deal with the mess? Baking powder helps create a crisp crust when these wings are roasted in the oven.

EASY | GLUTEN-FREE
TIME 1 hour, 30 minutes
(15 minutes active)
MAKES 6 to 8 servings

INGREDIENTS

- 3 pounds chicken wings (flats and drumettes)
- 3 teaspoons baking powder
- 1 teaspoon garlic powder
- 1 teaspoon onion powder
- ½ teaspoon cumin
- ½ teaspoon smoked paprika
- 1 tablespoon kosher salt
- 1½ teaspoons ground black pepper
  Cooking spray
- 2 canned chipotle peppers, minced, plus 2 tablespoons adobo sauce
- ⅓ cup maple syrup

1. Preheat oven to 250 F.
2. Pat chicken as dry as you can with paper towels. In a mixing bowl, stir together next 7 ingredients. Add chicken wings and toss to coat.
3. Line a rimmed baking sheet with foil and place a rack on top. Spray rack with cooking spray. Place wings on the rack in a single layer, skin-side up, so they're not touching. Bake for 30 minutes, then raise oven temperature to 425 F and continue baking for 40 to 50 minutes or until wings are golden.
4. In a microwave-safe bowl, combine chipotles, adobo and maple syrup. Heat for 1 minute. Pour sauce in a mixing bowl, add wings and toss to coat.

Pecan-Sausage Balls

Take these from freezer to oven!

EASY | MAKE-AHEAD
TIME 40 minutes
(15 minutes active)
MAKES 36 balls

INGREDIENTS

- ½ cup all-purpose flour
- ½ cup fine-ground cornmeal
- 2 teaspoons baking powder
- 1 tablespoon brown sugar
- 1 tablespoon rubbed sage
- ½ teaspoon kosher salt
- ½ teaspoon ground black pepper
- 1 (10-ounce) block cheddar cheese, grated
- 1 pound bulk spicy breakfast sausage
- 2 tablespoons grated onion
- 2 tablespoons buttermilk
- ½ cup pecans, finely chopped

1. Preheat oven to 350 F.
2. In a mixing bowl, whisk together first 7 ingredients. Add cheese and toss to coat. Add sausage, onion and buttermilk and mix with your hands to thoroughly combine.
3. Roll packed tablespoons of sausage mixture in pecans to coat and arrange on a parchment-lined baking sheet. Bake for 22 to 25 minutes until golden brown.

Fall-Fruit Sangria

Make this recipe a day ahead so the fruits infuse more flavor into the mix.

EASY | MAKE-AHEAD
TIME 20 minutes
(10 minutes active)
MAKES 6 to 8 servings

INGREDIENTS

- 1 (750-milliliter) bottle red wine (shiraz or zinfandel)
- ¼ cup apple brandy
- 1 cup apple juice
- 1 cup pomegranate juice
- ¼ cup honey
- 2 tablespoons water
- 2 cinnamon sticks
- 5 star anise
- 2 small apples, cored and thinly sliced
- 2 small pears, cored and thinly sliced
- 1 orange, thinly sliced

1. In a large pitcher, combine wine, brandy and fruit juices. In a microwave-safe liquid measuring cup, combine honey, water, cinnamon and anise, and heat for 30 seconds to 1 minute. Remove and set aside to cool and infuse, about 10 minutes.
2. Stir infused honey into wine mixture. Add fruit, chill and serve.

Fall-Fruit Sangria

Orange-Glazed
Pork Tenderloin
Party Sandwiches

Orange-Glazed Pork Tenderloin Party Sandwiches

Make these sandwiches an hour or so before your get-together. They can sit happily on the sideboard until guests arrive.

EASY | SPECIAL OCCASION
TIME 50 minutes
(15 minutes active)
MAKES 20 sandwiches

INGREDIENTS

- 2 pork tenderloins
- 1 teaspoon smoked paprika
- ½ teaspoon cayenne pepper
- 1 teaspoon cumin
- 1 teaspoon brown sugar
- 1 tablespoon kosher salt
- 2 teaspoons ground black pepper
- 1 tablespoon olive oil
- 1 cup orange marmalade, divided
- 1 head butter lettuce
- 1 (20-count) bag frozen par-baked yeast rolls (such as Sister Schubert), defrosted

1. Preheat oven to 375 F.
2. Pat tenderloins dry with paper towels. In a small bowl, stir together next 6 ingredients. Rub each tenderloin with spice mixture to coat.
3. In a 12-inch ovenproof skillet, add oil; heat over medium-high heat. When oil is shimmering, place tenderloins into pan; sear for about 2 minutes on each side. Place marmalade in a microwave-safe bowl and heat for 30 seconds to loosen. Flip tenderloins and spoon ½ cup marmalade evenly over each tenderloin.
4. Place skillet in oven and roast for 10 to 12 minutes or until a probe thermometer registers 145 F.

Remove tenderloins to a cutting board and rest for 15 minutes.
5. Reduce oven temperature to 350 F. Heat rolls for 8 to 10 minutes. Remove to wire rack.
6. When cooled, slice tenderloins into ¼-inch-thick slices and cut rolls in half horizontally.
7. To assemble sandwiches, top the base of each roll with 4 to 5 slices of pork, top with a lettuce leaf and a small spoonful of remaining marmalade. Serve warm or at room temperature.

Charred Onion Dip

Charring the onions in a dry skillet helps bring out smoky-sweet flavor.

EASY | FAMILY FRIENDLY | VEGETARIAN
TIME 30 minutes
(20 minutes active)
MAKES About 3 cups

INGREDIENTS

- 2 red onions, cut horizontally into ½-inch-thick slices
- 2 cups sour cream
- 1 tablespoon cream cheese, softened
- 3-4 dashes hot sauce
- 3-4 dashes Worcestershire sauce
- 2 tablespoons minced chives
- Juice and zest of ½ lemon
- ½ teaspoon kosher salt
- ½ teaspoon ground black pepper

1. Over medium-high heat, heat a large skillet. Add onions, working in batches if necessary. Char undisturbed for 8 to 10 minutes, then flip and cook for 8 to 10 minutes more. Remove onions to a plate to cool, then chop. (Reserve a few rings for garnish, if desired.)
2. In a mixing bowl, whisk together remaining ingredients. Stir in chopped onions. Serve with potato chips or crudités.

Refrigerate in an airtight container for up to 2 days.

Sweet & Spicy Candied Pecans

A hint of chili powder gives these sugared pecans some spicy depth.

EASY | MAKE-AHEAD | VEGETARIAN
TIME 1 hour, 10 minutes
(10 minutes active)
MAKES 3 cups

INGREDIENTS

- 1 egg white
- 1 tablespoon water
- 1 cup sugar
- 2 tablespoons cinnamon
- 1 teaspoon powdered ginger
- 1 teaspoon ground cloves
- ½ teaspoon nutmeg
- ½ teaspoon dark chili powder
- 1 teaspoon kosher salt
- 3 cups pecan halves
  Shortening, for greasing baking sheet

1. Preheat oven to 250 F.
2. In a mixing bowl, whip egg white and water until frothy. In a separate bowl, whisk together remaining ingredients (except pecans). Toss pecans in egg-white mixture until coated, then toss in the sugar mixture.
3. Grease a rimmed baking sheet. Spread nut mixture evenly over baking sheet. Bake for 1 hour, stirring every 20 minutes to prevent scorching. Cool, then store up to 1 week in an airtight container.

quick tip

For extra flavor and better browning, brush par-baked rolls with melted butter before warming.

quick tip

To defrost frozen shrimp, place desired amount in a bowl full of room-temperature water. They'll thaw in about 15 minutes.

Roasted Shrimp
With Spicy Pepper
Jelly & Cream Cheese

Roasted Shrimp With Spicy Pepper Jelly & Cream Cheese

Think of this easy layered appetizer as a less-fussy shrimp cocktail with a kick of heat.

EASY | SPECIAL OCCASION

TIME 30 minutes
(10 minutes active)

MAKES 8 to 10 servings

INGREDIENTS

- 1½   pounds peeled, deveined shrimp
- 2   tablespoons butter, melted
- 1   teaspoon Old Bay seasoning
- ¼   teaspoon kosher salt
- ¾   cup cream cheese, softened
- ¼–⅓ cup hot pepper jelly
    Minced chives, for garnish

1. Preheat oven to 400 F.
2. In a medium bowl, toss shrimp with butter, Old Bay and salt. Spread in an even layer on a rimmed baking sheet. Roast for 8 to 10 minutes. Set aside to cool.
3. Spread cream cheese on serving dish in an even layer. Spoon jelly on top, then tuck shrimp into the mixture. Garnish with chives to serve.

Marinated Olives & Feta Cheese

Serve as is for a savory snack, or chop the olives and use as a chunky dip or spread for crusty bread or crackers.

EASY | MAKE-AHEAD | VEGETARIAN

TIME 24 hours
(5 minutes active)

MAKES about 10 servings

INGREDIENTS

- 1 cup olive oil
- 3 cloves garlic, chopped
- Zest of 1 lemon
- 1 sprig rosemary
- 3 sprigs thyme
- ½ teaspoon crushed red pepper flakes
- 1 cup whole pitted Kalamata olives
- 1 cup whole pitted Sicilian Castelvetrano olives
- 8-10 ounces feta cheese, cubed

1. In a saucepan, add olive oil and next 5 ingredients and warm over medium heat; add olives and continue cooking for 2 to 3 minutes, swirling the pan. Remove from heat; let cool. Pour mixture into a bowl, jar or zip-close bag, and add cheese. Refrigerate and let marinate overnight for the best flavor.

Pepperoni-Sausage Skillet Pizza Dip

You might want to go ahead and double this crowd-pleasing recipe.

FAMILY FAVORITE | SPECIAL OCCASION
TIME 1 hour (10 minutes active)
MAKES About 8 servings

INGREDIENTS

- ¼ cup butter
- 1 teaspoon garlic powder, divided
- 1 teaspoon dried oregano, divided
- ¼ teaspoon crushed red pepper flakes
- 8-12 frozen dinner rolls (such as Rhodes), defrosted
- 1 (8-ounce) package cream cheese, softened
- 1 cup shredded part-skim mozzarella cheese, divided
- ½ cup mayonnaise
- ½ teaspoon dried basil
- ½ teaspoon kosher salt
- ½ teaspoon ground black pepper
- ½ cup pizza sauce, divided
- ¼ cup (¾ ounce) sliced pepperoni, divided
- ¼ cup (3 ounces) hot Italian sausage, cooked and crumbled, divided
- 1 jalapeño pepper, sliced into rounds, divided
- 2 tablespoons grated Parmesan cheese
- Fresh basil, for garnish

1. In a microwave-safe bowl, melt butter; stir in ½ teaspoon garlic powder, ½ teaspoon oregano and red pepper flakes. Dip rolls in butter mixture to coat and place around outer edge of a 12-inch oven-safe skillet. Cover skillet with a kitchen towel and let dough rise until almost doubled (about 30 minutes).

2. Preheat oven to 375 F. Bake until rolls are beginning to brown (about 10 minutes).

3. In a mixing bowl, combine cream cheese, ½ cup mozzarella, mayonnaise, basil, salt, pepper and remaining garlic powder and oregano. Spoon half of cheese mixture into center of skillet; top with half of the pizza sauce, half of the pepperoni, half of the sausage and half of the jalapeño, and ¼ cup mozzarella. Repeat layer. If you have any butter dip left, brush the tops of the rolls with it. Sprinkle with Parmesan. Bake for 10 to 12 minutes, loosely tenting with foil if needed to prevent over browning. Garnish with basil to serve.

Pepperoni-Sausage Skillet Pizza Dip

Sweet-Heat Jalapeño Poppers

Pimento cheese gives the stuffing extra flavor over traditional cream cheese alone. A finishing drizzle of honey sweetens the heat.

FAMILY FAVORITE | SPECIAL OCCASION
TIME 40 minutes
(20 minutes active)
MAKES 24 poppers

INGREDIENTS

- 4 ounces cream cheese, softened
- ½ cup premade pimento cheese
- ¼ cup sliced scallions
- 2 cloves garlic, minced
- 1 teaspoon kosher salt
- ½ teaspoon ground black pepper
- 12 fresh jalapeños, halved lengthwise and seeded
- 12 slices thin-cut bacon, halved crosswise
- Cooking spray
- Honey, for drizzling

1. Preheat oven to 450 F.
2. In a mixing bowl, stir together first 6 ingredients. Fill each pepper half with roughly 2 teaspoons of cheese mixture, being careful not to overstuff. Wrap each stuffed pepper with half a slice of bacon. Try to completely cover the cheese and have the end of the bacon slice wind up on the back of the pepper so it doesn't curl as it cooks.
3. Line a rimmed baking sheet with foil and place a rack on top.

quick tip
Look for jalapeños no longer than 3 inches with smooth, firm skin.

Spray rack with cooking spray. Place peppers so that rack cradles each to keep them upright. Bake for 20 to 25 minutes. Broil for 2 minutes to crisp the bacon, if needed. (Alternately, cook over medium-low on a charcoal or gas grill, nestling the peppers onto the grates as instructed. Watch carefully for flare-ups from the bacon.) Let cool for 5 minutes, then drizzle lightly with honey.

Crispy Buffalo Cauliflower Bites With Blue Cheese Dip

Frank's RedHot is the traditional hot sauce used in spicy Buffalo-style dishes, but feel free to substitute your preferred brand.

EASY | FAMILY FAVORITE | VEGETARIAN
TIME 30 minutes
(10 minutes active)
MAKES 6 to 8 servings

INGREDIENTS

- Cooking spray
- ¼ cup all-purpose flour
- 1 teaspoon kosher salt
- ¼ teaspoon ground black pepper
- 1/8 teaspoon cayenne pepper
- 1 head cauliflower, cut into florets
- 3 eggs
- ¼ cup whole milk
- 3 cups panko breadcrumbs
- ½ teaspoon garlic powder
- 2 tablespoons butter, melted
- ¼ cup hot sauce

1. Preheat oven to 375 F. Place a wire rack in a rimmed baking sheet; coat rack with cooking spray.
2. In a mixing bowl, stir together flour, salt and peppers. Add cauliflower and toss. In a second mixing bowl, whisk eggs and milk. In a wide, shallow dish, stir together panko and garlic powder. Transfer cauliflower, a few pieces at a time, from the flour mixture to the egg mixture, turning to coat, then roll in panko. Place breaded pieces on rack. Repeat until all pieces are coated. Bake for 20 minutes or until golden brown, turning occasionally to ensure even browning.
3. In a microwave-safe bowl, add butter and hot sauce. Microwave for 1 minute, then whisk to blend. Drizzle over baked cauliflower.

BLUE CHEESE DIP
In a mixing bowl, whisk together ¾ cup Greek yogurt, ¼ cup mayonnaise, zest and juice of half a lemon, ¼ teaspoon kosher salt and ¼ teaspoon ground black pepper. Stir in ½ cup blue cheese crumbles and 1 tablespoon chopped parsley or chives.

Chocolate Irish Cream Coffee

The whipped cream topping melts right into this indulgent after-dinner drink.

EASY | QUICK | SPECIAL OCCASION
TIME 5 minutes (all active)
MAKES 4 servings

INGREDIENTS

- 32 ounces (4 cups) brewed hot coffee
- 1½ tablespoons sugar
- 1½ tablespoons light brown sugar
- 2 tablespoons grated dark chocolate, plus more for garnish
- 6 ounces Irish whiskey
- 1 cup whipped cream

1. In a large mixing jug or pitcher, add coffee; stir in sugars and chocolate until dissolved. Add whiskey; stir to blend.
2. Divide mixture between 4 mugs. Dollop with whipped cream and sprinkle with grated chocolate.

**Sweet-Heat
Jalapeño Poppers**

Ham, Apple Butter & Cheddar Puff Pastry Triangles

For best results, defrost puff pastry overnight in the refrigerator. And work fast so it stays cool while you're rolling and filling. If needed, place the pan back in the refrigerator for 10 to 20 minutes before baking.

EASY | FAMILY FAVORITE | QUICK
TIME 30 minutes
(15 minutes active)
MAKES 18 servings

INGREDIENTS

 1 package (2 sheets) frozen puff pastry (such as Pepperidge Farm), defrosted
 3 tablespoons apple butter
 ¾ pounds smoked deli ham, sliced thin
 ¾ cup shredded sharp cheddar cheese
 1 egg, beaten, for egg wash
   Sea salt, for sprinkling

1. Preheat oven to 450 F.
2. Lightly flour a sheet of parchment paper. Unfold pastry sheets and gently roll to flatten. Spread apple butter over surface of 1 sheet, leaving 1-inch border around the edges. Lay ham slices on top of apple butter and sprinkle cheese evenly on top. Brush edges with egg wash and place second sheet of pastry on top of first, pressing edges lightly to adhere. Trim edges to neaten, brush entire surface with egg wash, cut several 2-inch slits in the surface to allow steam to escape, and sprinkle with sea salt.
3. Slide a sheet pan beneath the parchment; trim edges of paper even with pastry. Bake for 10 to 15 minutes or until pastry is puffed and golden. Cool on a rack for 10 minutes. To serve, cut evenly into 9 squares, then cut each diagonally to form triangles.

Slice & Bake Cheese Crisps

If you have time, leave butter and covered grated cheeses out overnight so they fully come to room temperature before mixing and baking.

MAKE-AHEAD | QUICK | VEGETARIAN
TIME 20 minutes
(10 minutes active)
MAKES 36 wafers

INGREDIENTS

 1 cup all-purpose flour
 ½ teaspoon kosher salt
 ½ teaspoon paprika
 ¼ teaspoon cayenne pepper
 ½ cup butter, softened
 2 cups sharp cheddar cheese, grated
 1 cup chopped, toasted pecans

1. In a mixing bowl, whisk together flour, salt, paprika and cayenne pepper to blend. In the bowl of a stand mixer fitted with a paddle attachment, add butter and cheese. Mix on medium speed until fluffy and well blended, about 5 minutes. Blend in flour mixture, then gently stir in pecans.
2. Place dough on a sheet of wax paper or plastic wrap and roll into a log, about 2 inches thick. Refrigerate overnight.
3. When ready to prepare, preheat oven to 350 F, unwrap and slice dough into ¼- to ½-inch-thick rounds. Bake on a parchment-lined baking sheet for 10 minutes or until crisp. Cool on a wire rack.

Ham, Apple Butter & Cheddar Puff Pastry Triangles

5 More Tasty Puff Pastry Sandwich Ideas

Puff pastry is a versatile base for any number of crowd-pleasing appetizers, like these sandwich triangles. Keep a packet tucked in your freezer for when you need to serve up something quick and easy for unexpected guests.

① BEEF & HORSERADISH
Spread pastry with 3 tablespoons creamy horseradish; top with ¾ pound sliced roast beef and ¾ cup shredded Swiss cheese.

② FIG & BLUE CHEESE
Spread pastry with 3 tablespoons fig preserves; top with ¾ pound sliced sugar-cured ham and ¾ cup crumbled blue cheese.

③ PEPPERONI PIZZA
Spread pastry with 2 tablespoons pizza sauce; top with 1 cup sliced pepperoni, 2 tablespoons chopped basil and ¾ cup shredded part-skim mozzarella cheese.

④ TURKEY & APRICOT
Spread pastry with 3 tablespoons apricot preserves; top with ¾ pound sliced smoked turkey and ¾ cup shredded Gruyère cheese.

⑤ HERBED CHEESE
Spread pastry with 3 tablespoons softened goat cheese; sprinkle with 3 tablespoons each chopped fresh parsley, basil and chives.

Smoky Lentil-
Sausage Soup,
page 32

quick tip

Before cooking, pour
lentils in a large bowl and
swirl with your fingers to
find any stems or stones.

chapter three

Soups & Stews

From rich, creamy fish chowder to velvet-smooth pureed squash soup or hearty, spicy chili, any of these super-comforting bowls will warm up a cool fall night.

Butternut Squash Soup With Herbed Croutons

Two shortcuts help bring this soup to the table fast—precut squash and jarred roasted garlic.

SPECIAL OCCASION | VEGETARIAN

TIME 45 minutes
(15 minutes active)
MAKES 4 to 6 servings

INGREDIENTS

- 1 tablespoon olive oil
- 1 small onion, diced
- 2 medium carrots, peeled and diced
- 4 cups peeled and cubed butternut squash
- 2 tablespoons drained jarred roasted garlic
- 1-1½ teaspoons fresh thyme leaves
- ¼ teaspoon turmeric
- 3 cups lower-sodium vegetable stock
- 3 cups half-and-half
   Pinch cayenne pepper
- ½ teaspoon salt
- ¼ teaspoon ground black pepper

1. In a large saucepan or Dutch oven over medium heat, warm oil. Add onion, carrot and squash; saute until softened, about 8 minutes.
2. Add remaining ingredients, stir and raise heat to medium-high until soup is steaming heavily and just about to boil, then reduce heat to low and simmer for 30 minutes. Test doneness of squash (if needed, simmer another 10 minutes) and puree with immersion blender until as smooth as possible. Top with croutons to serve.

HERBED CROUTONS

Preheat oven to 375 F. Remove crust from 6 to 8 pieces of day-old bread and cut into 1-inch squares. Pour ⅓ cup olive oil into a microwave-safe bowl; add 1 crushed garlic clove and 1 tablespoon fresh minced herbs, such as rosemary or thyme. Microwave on high for 1 minute, then strain and toss with bread. Spread on a rimmed baking sheet, sprinkle with salt and bake for 10 to 15 minutes.

Smoky Lentil-Sausage Soup

A finishing splash of apple cider vinegar brightens the flavor.

EASY | FAMILY FAVORITE

TIME 45 minutes
(15 minutes active)
MAKES 4 to 6 servings

INGREDIENTS

- 1 tablespoon olive oil
- 8 ounces smoked sausage, chopped
- 1 onion, peeled and diced
- 2 carrots, peeled and diced
- 2 celery ribs, diced
- 2 cloves garlic, minced
- ½ cup red wine
- 4 cups lower-sodium chicken stock
- 1 cup brown lentils
- 1 bay leaf
- 1 teaspoon kosher salt
- ¼ teaspoon ground black pepper
   Splash of apple cider vinegar

1. In a large Dutch oven over medium-high heat, warm oil. Add sausage and brown, stirring occasionally, about 5 to 7 minutes. Remove sausage and set aside. Add onion, carrot, celery and garlic to pan; saute until softened, about 6 to 8 minutes.
2. Add wine, scraping up any browned bits from the bottom of the pan. Cook for 1 to 2 minutes. Add chicken stock, lentils, bay leaf, salt and pepper, stirring to combine. Raise temperature to bring to a boil, then lower; cover and simmer for 30 minutes, stirring occasionally. Add sausage back to pot near end of cooking time. Thin with additional stock if needed. Just before serving, stir in a splash of vinegar.

Soup Beans

This rustic Appalachian dish is as simple to prepare as its name implies.

EASY | MAKE-AHEAD

TIME 24 hours
(20 minutes active)
MAKES 8 to 10 servings

INGREDIENTS

- 1 tablespoon canola oil
- 1 precooked ham steak (about 1 pound), chopped in small cubes
- 1 onion, diced (reserve 3 spoonfuls for garnish)
- 1-2 cloves garlic, minced
- 2 bay leaves
- 1 teaspoon smoked paprika
   Pinch cayenne pepper
- 2 teaspoons kosher salt, plus more to taste
- 1 teaspoon coarse-ground black pepper
- 1 pound dried pinto beans, soaked overnight

1. In a large Dutch oven over medium heat, warm oil; add ham and brown 5 to 7 minutes, stirring occasionally; remove with a slotted spoon and set aside. Add onion and garlic and saute until softened, about 5 to 7 minutes.
2. Return ham to the pot. Add bay leaves and spices, stirring to combine. Add drained beans and cover with water by 1 inch. Raise heat to bring to a boil, then lower; cover and simmer for 2 hours or until beans are tender (add water, half a cup at a time, if needed). Garnish with reserved onions to serve.

Butternut Squash Soup With Herbed Croutons

Roasted Tomato Soup

Bread helps give a velvety texture to this simple blend of tomatoes and cream.

FAMILY FAVORITE | VEGETARIAN

TIME 30 minutes
(10 minutes active)
MAKES 4 to 6 servings

INGREDIENTS

- 1 tablespoon butter
- 1 small onion, chopped
- 3 cloves garlic, minced
- 1 tablespoon sundried tomato paste
- 1 teaspoon dried oregano
- 1 slice day-old white bread, crusts removed, cut into cubes
- 2 (28-ounce) cans fire-roasted tomatoes
- 1 teaspoon kosher salt
- ¼ teaspoon ground black pepper
  Heavy cream, for garnish

1. In large Dutch oven over medium-high heat, warm butter. Saute onion until soft, about 5 minutes. Add garlic, tomato paste and oregano; cook 1 to 2 minutes.

2. Add bread, tomatoes with their juices, salt and pepper, stirring to combine. Raise heat to bring to boil, then reduce to simmer for 20 minutes.

3. Using an immersion blender, puree mixture (alternately, ladle a few cups at a time into a blender and puree in small batches, leaving the top vented and wrapped in a kitchen towel). Thin with vegetable stock, if needed. Swirl in heavy cream just before serving.

Beef & Butternut Squash Stew With Toasted-Almond Couscous

Look for jarred harissa, a North African blend of peppers, garlic and spices, in the international section of the grocery store.

EASY | SPECIAL OCCASION
TIME 1 hour (20 minutes active)
MAKES 6 servings

INGREDIENTS

- ½ cup all-purpose flour
- 1 teaspoon paprika
- 1 teaspoon cinnamon
- ½ teaspoon ground ginger
- 1 teaspoon kosher salt
- ½ teaspoon ground black pepper
- 1½ pounds beef shoulder roast, cut into 1-inch cubes
- 3 tablespoons canola oil
- 1 onion, diced
- 3 cloves garlic, minced
- 2 cups lower-sodium chicken stock
- 2 tablespoons jarred harissa, such as Mina
- 1 (14- to 16-ounce) can no-salt-added tomatoes
- 3 cups butternut squash, peeled and cubed
- 1 cinnamon stick
  Toasted Almond Couscous (recipe follows)
  Fresh cilantro, for garnish

1. In a large mixing bowl, whisk together flour, paprika, cinnamon, ginger, salt and pepper. Add beef and toss to coat, shaking off excess.
2. In a large Dutch oven over medium-high heat, warm oil. Sear beef for 8 to 10 minutes, stirring occasionally to ensure even browning and working in batches to avoid crowding the pan. Remove beef and set aside.
3. Lower heat to medium, add onion and saute until softened, about 5 minutes. Add garlic and cook for 1 minute more. Pour in chicken stock, harissa and tomatoes with their juices; stir to combine and raise heat to bring to a boil. Add beef, squash and cinnamon stick, reduce heat, cover and simmer for 40 minutes or until beef is cooked and squash is tender.
4. Remove cinnamon stick before serving. Serve over couscous and garnish with cilantro.

TOASTED ALMOND COUSCOUS

Prepare 1 cup couscous according to package directions. Fluff with a fork and set aside. Place ⅓ cup sliced almonds in a dry skillet over medium heat. Cook for 8 to 10 minutes, stirring or tossing frequently to prevent scorching. Gently stir almonds into couscous.

Chicken Cacciatore Stew

Increase the spice level with an extra teaspoon of crushed red pepper, if desired. Make this in an Instant Pot or slow cooker.

FAMILY FAVORITE | MAKE AHEAD
TIME 4 hours 30 minutes for slow cooker, 40 minutes for Instant Pot (30 minutes active)
MAKES 4 to 6 servings

INGREDIENTS

- ½ cup all-purpose flour
- 8 boneless, skinless chicken thighs, cut into 1-inch pieces
- 1 teaspoon kosher salt, plus more to season chicken
- 1 teaspoon ground black pepper, plus more to season chicken
- 3 tablespoons olive oil
- 2 small onions, chopped
- 2 small red bell peppers, seeded and chopped
- 6 cloves garlic, minced
- ½ cup red wine
- 2 tablespoons tomato paste
- 3 tablespoons capers, drained
- 1 teaspoon crushed red pepper
- 1½ teaspoons dried oregano
- 1 (14.5-ounce) can unsalted fire-roasted diced tomatoes), undrained
- 2 cups lower-sodium chicken stock
- 1 tablespoon cornstarch
  Fresh parsley, for garnish

1. Place flour in a mixing bowl; season chicken pieces with small amount of salt and pepper and toss in flour to coat, shaking off excess.
2. In a large skillet over medium-high heat, warm oil. Sear chicken for 5 to 7 minutes, stirring occasionally to ensure even browning and working in batches to avoid crowding the pan. Remove chicken and set aside.
3. Lower heat to medium; add onion, bell peppers and garlic and saute for 5 minutes. Add wine, bring to a boil, then simmer for 3 to 5 minutes. If using a slow cooker: Add chicken, onion mixture and remaining ingredients (except cornstarch and parsley), stir, cover and set to low for 4 hours. If making in an Instant Pot: Add chicken, onion mixture and remaining ingredients (except cornstarch and parsley), stir, cover and set to 10 minutes on high, sealed. Allow pressure to release naturally.
4. Ladle out ¼ cup cooking liquid. Add cornstarch and whisk to blend. Stir into stew, cover and allow to cook with residual heat for 5 to 7 minutes. Garnish with parsley.

Spicy White Bean & Chicken Chili

For less spice, omit the jalapeño.

EASY | FAMILY FAVORITE
TIME 40 minutes
(10 minutes active)
MAKES 4 to 6 servings

INGREDIENTS

- 1 tablespoon olive oil
- 1 small onion, peeled and chopped
- ½ jalapeño, seeded and minced
- 2 cloves garlic, peeled and minced
- 1 teaspoon cumin
- 1 teaspoon kosher salt
- ¼ teaspoon ground black pepper
- 1 (16-ounce) jar tomatillo salsa (such as Frontera)
- 4 cups lower-sodium chicken stock
- 2 (14- to 16-ounce) cans Great Northern beans, rinsed and drained (reserve 1 cup)
- 3 cups cooked, pulled chicken
- ¼ cup fresh cilantro, chopped, plus more for garnish
  Sour cream, for garnish

1. In a large Dutch oven over medium-high heat, warm oil. Saute onion, jalapeño and garlic until softened, about 6 to 8 minutes. Stir in cumin, salt, pepper, salsa, stock and beans and chicken.
2. Mash 1 cup reserved beans with a fork; stir into soup. Bring to a boil, then lower heat; cover and simmer for 30 minutes, stirring occasionally. Thin with additional stock if needed. Stir in cilantro. Garnish with additional cilantro and sour cream to serve.

Spicy White Bean & Chicken Chili

Creamy Mushroom Soup

When browned in butter, mushrooms take on a rich, almost meaty quality.

SPECIAL OCCASION | VEGETARIAN
TIME 40 minutes
(20 minutes active)
MAKES 4 to 6 servings

INGREDIENTS

- ½ cup butter
- 1 large shallot, diced
- 2 pounds sliced portobello mushrooms
- 1 tablespoon all-purpose flour
- 2 cloves garlic, minced
- 1 tablespoon sherry vinegar
- 2 cups vegetable stock
- 2-3 cups half-and-half
- 2-3 sprigs fresh thyme, plus more for garnish
- 1 teaspoon kosher salt
- ¼ teaspoon ground black pepper

1. In a large Dutch oven over medium-high heat, warm butter. Add shallot and saute for 2 to 3 minutes, then add mushrooms, working in batches to ensure even browning, about 5 to 7 minutes. When finished, return all mushrooms to the pan; sprinkle with flour and stir for 1 to 2 minutes.
2. Add garlic and vinegar and cook for 1 to 2 minutes more, scraping up any browned bits from the bottom of the pan. Stir in stock, half-and-half, thyme, salt and pepper; cook for 5 minutes, then lower heat and simmer for 20 minutes. Garnish with fresh thyme to serve.

**Creamy
Mushroom Soup**

quick tip

To keep mushrooms firm when sauteing, avoid seasoning with salt. That way, they won't release water, which prevents caramelization.

Hearty Beef Chili

No beans around in this spin on Texas-style chili!

FAMILY FAVORITE | MAKE AHEAD

TIME 8 hours 30 minutes for slow cooker, 1 hour for Instant Pot (30 minutes active)

MAKES 4 to 6 servings

INGREDIENTS

- ½ cup all-purpose flour
- 2½ pounds beef chuck roast, cut into 1-inch cubes
  Salt and ground black pepper, to taste
- 3 tablespoons canola oil
- 1 large red onion, diced
- 6 cloves garlic, minced
- 1 poblano pepper, seeded and chopped
- 1½ tablespoons chili powder
- 1½ teaspoons cumin
- 1 cinnamon stick
- 12 ounces dark beer
- 1 (12-ounce) can diced tomatoes with green chiles (such as Ro*Tel), drained
- 2 cups beef stock
- 3 tablespoons dark brown sugar
- 2 canned chipotle chiles in adobo sauce, minced
- 2 teaspoons dried oregano
- ⅓ cup chopped fresh cilantro, plus more for garnish
- 1 tablespoon cornstarch
  Sliced jalapeños, for garnish

1. Place flour in a mixing bowl; season beef pieces with salt and pepper and toss in flour to coat, shaking off excess.

2. In a large Dutch oven over medium-high heat, warm oil. Sear beef for 8 to 10 minutes, stirring occasionally to ensure even browning and working in batches to avoid crowding the pan. Remove beef from pan and set aside.

3. Lower heat to medium, add onion, garlic, poblano and spices and saute for 5 minutes. Add beer, bring to a boil, then simmer for 3 to 5 minutes. If using a slow cooker: Add beef, onion mixture, canned tomatoes, stock, sugar, chiles, oregano and cilantro; stir, cover and set to low for 8 hours. If cooking in an Instant Pot: Add beef, onion mixture, canned tomatoes, stock, sugar, chiles, oregano and cilantro; stir, cover and set to 30 minutes on high, sealed. Allow pressure to release naturally.

4. Remove cinnamon stick. Ladle out 1/4 cup cooking liquid. Add cornstarch and whisk to blend. Stir into stew, cover and allow to cook with residual heat for 5 to 7 minutes. Garnish to serve.

Chicken & Rice Soup With Lemon Gremolata

Rotisserie chicken helps bring this soup to the table quickly.

EASY | QUICK

TIME 1 hour (20 minutes active)

MAKES 6 to 8 servings

INGREDIENTS

- 2 tablespoons olive oil
- 1 onion, diced
- 1 leek, halved and thinly sliced
- 3 carrots, peeled and sliced into rounds
- 2 celery ribs, diced
- 2 cloves garlic, minced

---

quick tip

Cooking rice directly in the soup's broth helps it absorb flavor.

- 3-4 sprigs fresh thyme
- 2 tablespoons parsley, minced, plus more for garnish
- 1 tablespoon fresh sage, minced
- 1 bay leaf
- 1 teaspoon kosher salt
- ½ teaspoon ground black pepper
- 2 cups shredded cooked rotisserie chicken
- 6 cups lower-sodium chicken stock
  Zest and juice of ½ lemon
- 1 cup long-grain white rice

1. In a large Dutch oven or stockpot over medium-high heat, warm oil. Saute onion, leek, carrots and celery until softened, about 5 to 7 minutes. Add garlic, thyme, parsley, sage, bay leaf, salt and pepper and stir to combine.

2. Stir in chicken. Pour in chicken stock, scraping up any browned bits from the bottom on the pan, and stir in lemon zest and juice, and rice. Raise heat to bring to a boil, then simmer for 30 to 40 minutes, covered, until chicken and rice are fully cooked. If desired, add more broth. Top with gremolata (see below) and garnish with parsley to serve.

LEMON GREMOLATA

In a small bowl, combine ½ cup finely minced parsley with zest of 1 lemon and 2 finely minced garlic cloves.

Sausage & Shrimp Gumbo

Making the roux—the base for many traditional Creole dishes—is the only time-consuming part of this recipe.

FAMILY FAVORITE | SPECIAL OCCASION

TIME 1 hour, 30 minutes (30 minutes active)

MAKES 8 to 10 servings

INGREDIENTS

- ¼ cup plus 2 tablespoons vegetable oil
- ¼ cup plus 2 tablespoons all-purpose flour
- 1 large onion, chopped
- 2 celery ribs, chopped
- 1 green bell pepper, seeded and chopped
- 4 cloves garlic, minced
- 1½ teaspoons kosher salt
- 1 teaspoon ground black pepper
- 3 cups frozen sliced okra
- 1 (14- to 16-ounce) can no-salt-added chopped tomatoes
- 6 cups lower-sodium chicken stock
- 2 bay leaves
- 12 ounces smoked andouille sausage (such as Aidells), sliced
- 1½ pounds peeled and deveined shrimp, with tails removed
  Parsley, for garnish
  Cooked rice, for serving

1. In a large Dutch oven or stockpot over medium heat, warm oil; add flour and whisk to make roux. Continue whisking until roux becomes the color of milk chocolate, about 20 minutes.

2. Add onion, celery, bell pepper, garlic, salt and pepper and stir to combine. Continue cooking, stirring often, until vegetables are softened, about 10 minutes. Add okra, tomatoes and their juices, stock, bay leaves and sausage, stirring to combine.

3. Raise heat to bring to boil, then reduce to simmer for 1 hour, stirring occasionally.

4. About 10 minutes before serving, raise heat to medium and stir in shrimp. Remove bay leaves. Garnish with parsley; serve over rice.

quick tip
Canned chipotle chiles in adobo sauce add wonderfully smoky depth; look for them in the international or Mexican sections of your grocery store.

Hearty Beef Chili

quick tip

You can substitute any variety of firm, white-fleshed fish that will hold its shape during cooking.

Creamy Fish Chowder With Buttery Old Bay Oyster Crackers

Fall Vegetable Minestrone

To make it vegan, omit the cheese.

SPECIAL OCCASION | VEGETARIAN

TIME 1 hour (20 minutes active)

MAKES 8 to 10 servings

INGREDIENTS

2 (14- to 16-ounce) cans cannellini beans
2 tablespoons olive oil
1 onion, diced
3 carrots, peeled and diced
2 celery ribs, diced
2 cups butternut squash, cubed
3 cloves garlic, minced
1 cup green beans, chopped into 1-inch pieces
1 teaspoon dried oregano
1 teaspoon dried basil
1 teaspoon dried thyme
2 teaspoons kosher salt
½ teaspoon ground black pepper
1 cup white wine
6 cups lower-sodium vegetable broth, plus more if needed
1 (14- to 16-ounce) can chopped tomatoes
½ small russet potato, peeled
¾ cup uncooked ditalini pasta
1 bay leaf
2 cups fresh baby spinach leaves
½ cup Parmesan cheese, grated, plus more for garnish
¼ cup parsley, minced, plus more for garnish

1. Rinse beans and set aside.
2. In a large Dutch oven over medium-high heat, warm oil. Saute onion, carrots, celery and squash until softened, about 8 minutes. Add garlic, green beans, oregano, basil, thyme, salt and pepper and stir to combine. Pour in wine, broth and tomatoes with their juices.
3. Grate potato directly into the liquid. Add pasta and bay leaf.

Fall Vegetable Minestrone

Raise heat to bring to a boil, then simmer for 30 to 40 minutes, covered, until squash is tender. If desired, add more broth. Remove bay leaf and stir in spinach, Parmesan and parsley 5 minutes before serving. Garnish with additional Parmesan and parsley.

Creamy Fish Chowder With Buttery Old Bay Oyster Crackers

The crunch of spiced crackers contrasts well with this rich soup—perfect for a crisp day!

EASY | FAMILY FAVORITE

TIME 45 minutes (15 minutes active)

MAKES 6 servings

INGREDIENTS

4 strips bacon, diced
1 medium onion, diced
2 celery ribs, diced
½ small fennel bulb, peeled and diced (save fronds for garnish)
1 large Yukon Gold potato, diced
1 bay leaf
1-3 sprigs thyme
3 cups fish or vegetable stock
1 cup whole milk
1 cup half-and-half
1 teaspoon salt
½ teaspoon ground black pepper
1 pound cod or halibut fillets, cut into 1-inch cubes
   Hot sauce and Buttery Old Bay Oyster Crackers (recipe follows), for serving

1. In a large Dutch oven over medium heat, saute bacon until browned, about 5 minutes. Add onion, celery, fennel and potato and saute until softened, about 8 minutes.
2. Add remaining ingredients (except fish), stir and raise heat to medium-high until soup is steaming heavily and about to boil, then reduce heat to low, add fish and simmer for 30 minutes uncovered. Remove thyme stems. Garnish with fennel fronds. Serve with hot sauce and crackers.

BUTTERY OLD BAY OYSTER CRACKERS

Preheat oven to 350 F. In a large microwavable bowl, microwave ¼ cup butter until melted. Stir in 2 teaspoons Old Bay seasoning and toss with 4 cups oyster crackers. Spread on a rimmed baking sheet and bake for 20 to 30 minutes, tossing occasionally.

Flank Steak
With Romesco
Sauce & Grilled
Caesar Salad,
page 44

quick tip

For tender, juicy
roasted or grilled meats,
be sure to let them
rest before slicing.

chapter four

Main Dishes

Quick-cooking weeknight dinners, special-occasion entrees and more.

Flank Steak With Romesco Sauce & Grilled Caesar Salad

To make this recipe even easier, substitute your favorite bottled balsamic vinaigrette salad dressing for the overnight marinade. Make the sauce ahead, too; it will keep, refrigerated in an airtight container, for up to 1 week.

EASY | MAKE-AHEAD

TIME 12 hours (or more), 30 minutes (30 minutes active)

MAKES 4 servings

INGREDIENTS
FOR STEAK

- ½ cup balsamic vinegar
- 2 tablespoons Dijon mustard
- 2 cloves garlic, minced
- 1 tablespoon chopped rosemary
- 1 teaspoon kosher salt
- ½ teaspoon ground black pepper
- 1 cup olive oil, plus more for grilling
- 1 (2-pound) flank steak

FOR SAUCE

- ½ cup smoked almonds (such as Blue Diamond)
- 2 cloves garlic, peeled
- ½ cup jarred roasted red bell peppers, drained (about 1 whole pepper)
- 2 tablespoons tomato paste
- 2 tablespoons chopped parsley
- 2 tablespoons sherry vinegar
- 1 teaspoon smoked paprika
- ¼ teaspoon kosher salt
- ¼ teaspoon ground black pepper
- ¼ teaspoon cayenne pepper
- ¼ cup extra-virgin olive oil

1. To make marinade: in a mixing bowl, whisk together vinegar, mustard, garlic, rosemary, salt and pepper; slowly pour in oil while whisking. In a wide, shallow dish, add steak; pour marinade on top. Cover and refrigerate overnight.

2. To make the sauce: In a food processor, add all sauce ingredients except olive oil. Blend for 1 to 2 minutes, then drizzle oil through the open tube until sauce is smooth.

3. Heat a grill over high heat, or a seasoned grill pan over medium-high heat. Remove steak from marinade, shaking off excess, and grill for 10 to 12 minutes, flipping once, or until a probe thermometer registers 125 F.

4. Remove steak to a cutting board and loosely tent with foil; rest for 10 minutes before slicing crosswise against the grain. Serve with sauce and Grilled Caesar Salad (recipe follows).

GRILLED CAESAR SALAD

Slice 2 hearts of romaine lettuce in half lengthwise. Drizzle lightly with about 2 tablespoons of oil from a jar or tin of anchovies, season each with a pinch of kosher salt and ground black pepper. Place cut-side down on hot grill grates or grill pan for 2 minutes, then remove. Finely chop 3 to 4 anchovies and scatter over lettuce; top each with ¼ cup finely shaved Parmesan cheese.

Roasted Cauliflower Tacos With Quick Pickled Onions

Once the spiced cauliflower is roasted, this easy all-vegetable entree comes together quickly.

EASY | FAMILY FAVORITE | VEGETARIAN

TIME 45 minutes (15 minutes active)

MAKES 4 servings

**Roasted Cauliflower Tacos
With Quick Pickled Onions**

INGREDIENTS

1	head cauliflower, cut into florets
2	tablespoons olive oil
1	teaspoon cumin
½	teaspoon turmeric
⅛	teaspoon cayenne pepper
½	teaspoon kosher salt
¼	teaspoon ground black pepper
¾	cup roasted tomatillo salsa (such as Frontera)
12	flour tortillas, warmed Fresh cilantro, for garnish

1. Preheat oven to 425 F.
2. In a large mixing bowl, toss cauliflower with oil and spices. Place on a rimmed baking sheet and roast for 20 to 25 minutes, turning occasionally, until tender.
3. Spread 1 tablespoon salsa on each tortilla and top with roasted cauliflower; garnish with additional salsa, if desired, plus cilantro and Quick Pickled Onions (recipe follows).

QUICK PICKLED ONIONS
In a saucepan over medium-low heat, warm ½ cup red wine vinegar, 1 tablespoon sugar and 1 teaspoon kosher salt, stirring until sugar and salt is dissolved, about 2 to 3 minutes. Remove from heat, add 1 red onion, sliced vertically, and let sit at room temperature for 1 hour. Refrigerate in an airtight container for up to 2 weeks.

quick tip
To char tortillas, use tongs to place directly on grates over a medium-high gas flame one at a time for about 1 minute per side, watching carefully to avoid burning.

Shrimp & Grits

If you can't find stone-ground grits for this traditional Low Country dish, you can substitute polenta.

──────────

EASY | FAMILY FAVORITE

TIME 45 minutes (20 active)

MAKES 4 servings

INGREDIENTS

- 4 slices bacon, chopped
- 1 cup sliced mushrooms
- 1 green bell pepper, seeded and chopped
- 1½ pounds raw shrimp, peeled and deveined
- 3 tablespoons all-purpose flour
- 1 clove garlic, minced
- ½ teaspoon kosher salt
- ¼ teaspoon ground black pepper
- 1 tablespoon tomato paste
- ½ cup lower-sodium chicken stock
- Zest and juice of half a lemon
- 1 cup stone-ground grits, prepared according to package directions (about 4 cups)
- 4 scallions, thinly sliced, for garnish

1. In a large skillet over medium-high heat, brown bacon, stirring occasionally, about 5 to 7 minutes. Remove with a slotted spoon and set aside on a paper-towel-lined plate.

2. Add mushrooms and bell pepper to skillet and saute for 5 minutes.

3. In a mixing bowl, toss shrimp with flour, shaking off any excess, and add to skillet, along with garlic, salt and pepper. Continue to cook, stirring often, for 3 to 5 minutes more or until shrimp are cooked through.

4. In a small bowl, whisk together tomato paste and stock; stir into skillet with reserved bacon, lemon zest and juice. Cook for 1 to 2 minutes more. Serve over grits; garnish with scallions.

Baked Pork Chops & Brown-Sugar Apples

This classic fall combination is all baked together in one dish.

──────────

EASY | FAMILY FAVORITE

TIME 1 hour, 5 minutes (15 minutes active)

MAKES 8 servings

INGREDIENTS

- 2 tablespoons unsalted butter
- 8 center-cut, bone-in pork chops, about ½-inch thick
- 1½ teaspoons kosher salt
- ½ teaspoon ground black pepper
- ½ teaspoon rubbed sage
- 4 apples, cored and sliced
- ¼ cup light brown sugar
- 2 tablespoons all-purpose flour
- 1 cup lower-sodium chicken broth
- ½ teaspoon apple cider vinegar
- ½ cup golden raisins

1. Preheat oven to 350 F.

2. In a large skillet over medium-high heat, melt butter. Add pork and brown on both sides, about 2 to 3 minutes, working in batches; place chops in a 13x9-inch baking dish. (Set skillet with pan drippings aside.) Sprinkle chops with salt, pepper and sage. Top with apples. Sprinkle with brown sugar.

3. Return skillet to medium-low heat. Whisk flour into pan drippings, along with broth and vinegar. Whisk until thickened, about 2 to 3 minutes. Stir in raisins and pour sauce into baking dish. Bake for 40 to 50 minutes.

5 More Great Grits Pairings

Rich and creamy, grits can be the base for many hearty, warming meals.

──────────

❶ CHICKEN & BLACK BEANS Toss 2 cups of shredded rotisserie chicken with a few spoonfuls of your favorite salsa. Warm 1 (14- to 16-ounce) can of drained black beans with ½ cup lower-sodium chicken stock, ½ teaspoon cumin, and salt and pepper to taste. Spoon over cooked grits; top with shredded cheddar.

❷ BARBECUE PORK Melt shredded cheddar into cooked grits; top with pulled pork (see page 52) and garnish with sliced scallions.

❸ LEFTOVER CHILI Ladle warm chili over servings of cooked grits. Garnish with shredded cheddar, sliced jalapeños, crumbled tortilla chips and fresh cilantro.

❹ CARAMELIZED ONIONS Slowly saute 2 sliced onions in 2 tablespoons of butter over low heat until fully caramelized, about 30 to 40 minutes, stirring often. Spoon over cooked grits; garnish with fresh thyme.

❺ MUSHROOMS Saute 1 pound sliced mushrooms and 1 teaspoon fresh thyme in 2 tablespoons unsalted butter over medium-high heat until nicely browned (about 8 to 10 minutes). Add ½ cup red wine, then reduce by half; season to taste, and spoon over servings of cooked grits. Top with grated Parmesan.

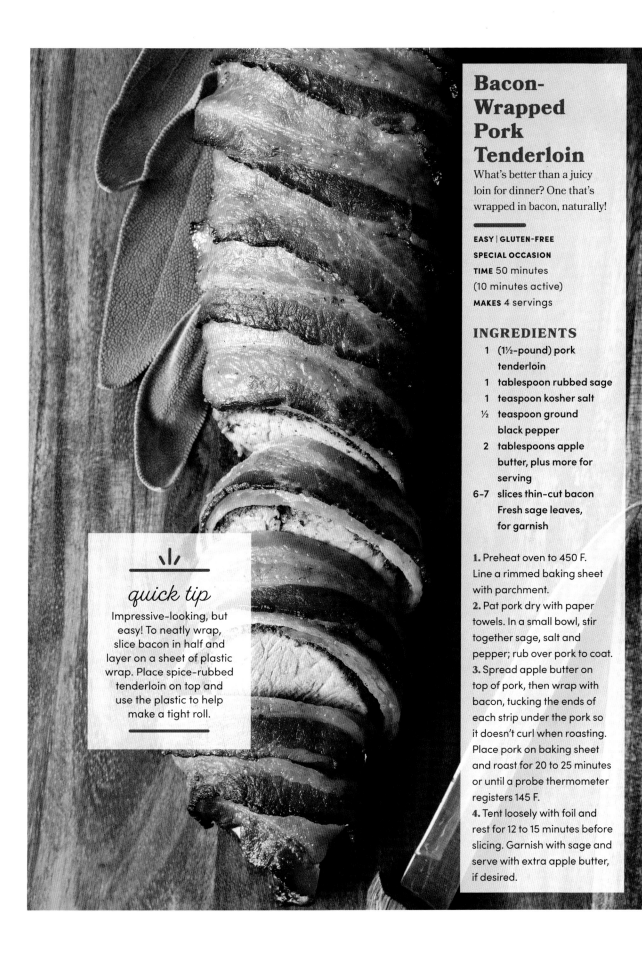

Bacon-Wrapped Pork Tenderloin

What's better than a juicy loin for dinner? One that's wrapped in bacon, naturally!

EASY | GLUTEN-FREE
SPECIAL OCCASION
TIME 50 minutes
(10 minutes active)
MAKES 4 servings

INGREDIENTS

- 1 (1½-pound) pork tenderloin
- 1 tablespoon rubbed sage
- 1 teaspoon kosher salt
- ½ teaspoon ground black pepper
- 2 tablespoons apple butter, plus more for serving
- 6-7 slices thin-cut bacon
  Fresh sage leaves, for garnish

1. Preheat oven to 450 F. Line a rimmed baking sheet with parchment.
2. Pat pork dry with paper towels. In a small bowl, stir together sage, salt and pepper; rub over pork to coat.
3. Spread apple butter on top of pork, then wrap with bacon, tucking the ends of each strip under the pork so it doesn't curl when roasting. Place pork on baking sheet and roast for 20 to 25 minutes or until a probe thermometer registers 145 F.
4. Tent loosely with foil and rest for 12 to 15 minutes before slicing. Garnish with sage and serve with extra apple butter, if desired.

quick tip

Impressive-looking, but easy! To neatly wrap, slice bacon in half and layer on a sheet of plastic wrap. Place spice-rubbed tenderloin on top and use the plastic to help make a tight roll.

Deep-Dish Spinach-Artichoke Pie

Par-baking a double-layer pastry with an egg wash helps ensure a crisp crust that's sturdy enough to hold the pie's rich filling.

SPECIAL OCCASION | VEGETARIAN
TIME 2 hours (40 minutes active)
MAKES 8 servings

INGREDIENTS

- 1 (14.1-ounce) package refrigerated pie dough (2 crusts)
- 5 eggs, divided
- 4 tablespoons butter, divided
- 2 pounds fresh spinach, washed and dried
- 2 cups heavy cream
- ½ teaspoon dried basil
- ¼ teaspoon nutmeg
- ½ teaspoon kosher salt
- ½ teaspoon ground black pepper
- Pinch cayenne pepper
- Zest of half a lemon
- 1 (12-ounce) jar marinated artichokes, drained and chopped
- 1 cup crumbled feta cheese
- ⅓ cup grated Parmesan cheese

1. Preheat oven to 400 F.
2. On a lightly floured surface, stack dough rounds together to create a double thickness and roll together to a 12-inch circle. Drape pastry into an 8- or 9-inch deep-dish pie plate or springform pan, pressing the dough into the corners and up the sides; crimp as desired. Lightly press a piece of foil into the pan and weight down with pie weights or dried beans. Bake for 10 minutes; remove from oven and carefully remove weights and foil.
3. Lightly prick the dough with a fork to prevent bubbling and return to oven. Bake 8 to 10 minutes more until set. Meanwhile, in a small bowl, beat 1 egg. Remove crust from oven and brush the bottom with egg to completely coat. Bake 2 to 3 minutes more. Remove from oven and set aside to cool.
4. In a large skillet over medium heat, melt 2 tablespoons butter. Add half the spinach and wilt, turning frequently, about 3 minutes; repeat with remaining butter and spinach. Drain thoroughly.
5. In a large bowl, whisk together remaining 4 eggs, cream, basil, nutmeg, salt, pepper, cayenne and lemon zest. Add drained spinach, artichokes and feta, stirring to combine. Spoon spinach mixture into prepared pie shell. Top with Parmesan. Bake 45 to 50 minutes or until beginning to brown, tenting pie shell edges with foil if needed to prevent overbrowning. Cool on a rack for 20 minutes before slicing.

Chipotle Chicken Taquitos With Creamy Avocado Dip

A simple stir-together blend of smoky chipotle peppers and creamy refried beans provides a flavorful base for rotisserie chicken. Swap corn for flour tortillas to make it gluten-free.

EASY | FAMILY FAVORITE | QUICK
TIME 25 minutes (all active)
MAKES 4 servings

INGREDIENTS

- 1 cup canned refried beans, divided
- 1 chipotle pepper in adobo sauce, finely minced
- ½ cup sour cream
- 1 teaspoon cumin
- 1 teaspoon chili powder
- ½ teaspoon salt
- 1 pound pulled rotisserie chicken
- 16 (6-inch) flour tortillas, warmed
- 1 cup shredded cheddar cheese, divided
- ¼ cup canola oil
- 1 tomato, chopped, for garnish
- 1 shallot, minced, for garnish
- ½ cup chopped fresh cilantro, for garnish

1. Preheat oven to 400 F. Line a rimmed baking sheet with parchment.
2. In a small bowl, stir together beans and chipotle.
3. In a large mixing bowl, whisk together sour cream, cumin, chili powder and salt. Add chicken and toss to coat.
4. Spread each tortilla with 1 tablespoon bean mixture, top with ¼ cup chicken mixture and 1 tablespoon cheese. Roll tightly and place seam-side down on baking sheet. Repeat with remaining tortillas. Brush tops with oil and bake for 15 minutes or until crisp and golden brown.
5. In a small bowl, toss together tomato, shallot and cilantro for a garnish or topping. Serve with Creamy Avocado Dip (recipe follows) on the side.

CREAMY AVOCADO DIP
Place two peeled and seeded avocados in a food processor. Add ¾ cup Greek yogurt, zest and juice of half a lime, 1 teaspoon cumin and ¼ teaspoon kosher salt. Pulse until blended. For a spicy version, add ½ of a jalapeño pepper, seeded and chopped.

Mushroom- & Walnut- Stuffed Acorn Squash

Squash stuffed with quinoa and mushrooms makes for a hearty vegetarian entree.

EASY | VEGETARIAN

TIME 1 hour 15 minutes (25 active)

MAKES 6 servings

INGREDIENTS

- ½ cup quinoa, rinsed
- 3 acorn squash, unpeeled, halved lengthwise and seeded
- 3 tablespoons olive oil, divided
- 2 teaspoons kosher salt
- 1 teaspoon ground black pepper
- 8 ounces sliced baby bella mushrooms
- 1 onion, peeled and diced
- 1 carrot, peeled and diced
- 2 ribs celery, diced
- ¼ cup chopped walnuts
- 1 tablespoon fresh sage, chopped
- ½ cup Parmesan cheese

1. In a medium saucepan over medium-high heat, add quinoa and 1 cup water; when water simmers, turn heat to medium-low and simmer until tender, about 15 minutes. Drain and set aside to cool.

2. Preheat oven to 350 F.

3. Place squash halves, cut-side up, on a rimmed baking sheet. Brush with 1 tablespoon oil and sprinkle with salt and pepper. Set aside.

4. In a large skillet over medium-high heat, warm 1 tablespoon oil. Saute mushrooms 10 minutes; remove from pan. Add remaining oil to skillet; saute onion, carrot and celery until softened, about 5 to 7 minutes.

5. In a mixing bowl, stir together prepared quinoa, cooked vegetables, walnuts and sage. Spoon quinoa mixture into squash cavities, sprinkle with Parmesan and bake for 40 to 50 minutes, or until squash is tender when pierced with a fork.

quick tip

To help squash stand upright while baking, cut a small thin slice from the bottom side before stuffing.

Guinness-
Braised
Short Ribs

Guinness-Braised Short Ribs

This recipe is worth the time it takes to cook in the oven instead of a slow cooker or Instant Pot; the sauce reduces and thickens, and the short ribs continue to brown. Bones add flavor and body as the dish cooks, but boneless short ribs work, too.

GLUTEN-FREE | SPECIAL OCCASION

TIME 2 hours, 30 minutes
(30 minutes active)

MAKES 4 to 6 servings

INGREDIENTS

- 2 tablespoons olive oil
- 5 pounds beef short ribs, about 8 total, with or without bones
- 1 tablespoon kosher salt
- 2 teaspoons ground black pepper
- 1 large onion, chopped
- 3 ribs celery, sliced
- 6 carrots, peeled and cut into 2-inch-long pieces
- 2 (8-ounce) packages baby bella mushrooms, cleaned and quartered
- 3 cloves garlic, minced
- 4 cups red wine, divided
- 2 cups beef stock
- 1 (28-ounce) can crushed fire-roasted tomatoes, such as Muir Glen
- 1 (11.2-ounce) bottle Guinness draught stout
- 2 sprigs fresh rosemary
  Fresh parsley, for garnish

1. Preheat oven to 400 F.
2. In a large Dutch oven over medium-high heat, warm oil. Season short ribs with salt and pepper and brown on each side, about 2 to 3 minutes, working in batches if needed. Set ribs aside.
3. Add onion, celery, carrots and mushrooms to the Dutch oven; saute until softened, about 6 to 8 minutes. Add garlic and cook 1 minute more. Pour 1 cup of wine into the pot to deglaze, scraping up any browned bits. Return short ribs to the pot, along with any collected juices. Add remaining wine, stock, tomatoes, beer and rosemary, stirring to combine.
4. Cover Dutch oven and bake, covered, for 1 hour. Uncover, stir and bake for 1 hour more. Remove from oven; remove and discard rosemary stems. Serve over mashed potatoes or polenta; garnish with parsley or more rosemary.

Baked Pork Chops With Wild Rice

Take full time-saving advantage and use the sage-flavored spice packet inside the boxed rice mix.

FAMILY FAVORITE | GLUTEN-FREE

TIME 40 minutes (10 minutes active)

MAKES 4 servings

INGREDIENTS

- 2 tablespoons butter, divided
- 4 boneless center-cut pork chops
- ½ teaspoon kosher salt
- ¼ teaspoon ground black pepper
- ½ small onion, peeled and chopped
- 1 celery rib, chopped
- ½ cup chopped walnuts
- ½ cup dried cranberries
- 1 (6-ounce) package long grain and wild rice blend (such as Ben's Original)
- 1 cup lower-sodium chicken stock

1. Preheat oven to 350 F.

2. In a skillet over medium-high heat, warm butter; season pork chops with salt and pepper and brown on both sides, about 3 minutes; set aside.

3. Add remaining butter to skillet and saute onion and celery until softened, about 5 minutes. Stir in nuts and cranberries.

4. Pour onion mixture, rice and spice packet into an 8-inch square baking dish; add stock and stir to combine. Top with pork, wrap baking dish with foil, and bake for 30 minutes or until a probe thermometer registers 145 F.

Sweet Heat Roasted Ribs

Think of these fall-off-the-bone oven-roasted ribs as a rainy-day substitute for traditional smoked.

▬▬▬▬▬▬

GLUTEN-FREE | SPECIAL OCCASION
TIME 2 hours (20 minutes active)
MAKES 4 to 6 servings

INGREDIENTS

- 2 racks baby back ribs, about 3½ pounds total
- 4 cloves garlic, mashed into a paste
- ⅓ cup molasses
- 2 tablespoons apple cider vinegar
- 1½ tablespoons salt, divided
- ½ tablespoon ground black pepper
- 2 teaspoons cayenne pepper

1. Preheat oven to 425 F.
2. Pat ribs dry with paper towels. In a small bowl, mix remaining ingredients. Rub about 3 tablespoons of the mixture evenly over ribs; reserve the rest. (For deeper flavor, do this 1 day ahead, wrap ribs tightly in plastic wrap, and refrigerate overnight.)

3. Pour 1 cup water into the base of a roasting pan. Arrange ribs on a wire rack and wrap rack tightly with foil and place in pan. Bake for 1½ hours or until ribs are tender.
4. Carefully remove ribs from rack and place on a rimmed baking sheet; broil for 3 to 5 minutes until lightly charred.
5. Remove ribs to a rack and let rest for 10 minutes before separating into individual servings. Drizzle with remaining sauce.

Pulled Pork With Brown Sugar Barbecue Sauce

This set-it and forget-it recipe feeds a big crowd. You can make it in an Instant Pot or slow cooker.

▬▬▬▬▬▬

EASY | GLUTEN-FREE
TIME 9 hours slow cooker/ 2½ hours Instant Pot (15 minutes active)
MAKES 12 to 15 servings

INGREDIENTS

- ¼ cup light brown sugar
- 2 tablespoons kosher salt
- 1 tablespoon ground black pepper
- 1 tablespoon cumin
- 1 tablespoon smoked paprika
- 1 teaspoon cayenne pepper
- 1 teaspoon onion powder
- 1 teaspoon garlic powder
- 1 (5- to 6-pound) pork butt
- 2 tablespoons canola oil
- 1½ cups lower-sodium chicken stock
- 1 bay leaf

1. Make the spice rub: In a small bowl, mix sugar, salt, pepper, cumin, paprika, cayenne, onion powder and garlic powder. Pat pork dry with paper towels. Rub spice mixture evenly over pork. (For deeper flavor, do this 1 day ahead; wrap pork in plastic wrap and refrigerate overnight.)
2. In a large Dutch oven over medium-high heat, warm oil. Add pork and sear on all sides, about 2 to 3 minutes each.
3. Place pork in Instant Pot or slow cooker. Pour stock into Dutch oven to deglaze, scraping up any browned bits, about 1 minute. Pour this liquid into Instant Pot or slow cooker. Add bay leaf. If cooking in an Instant Pot: Set to manual and cook on high for 1 hour, 15 minutes. Release pressure naturally. If using a slow cooker: Set to high and cook for 8 hours.
4. Remove pork from Instant Pot or slow cooker and place in a large bowl. Shred meat with two forks. Drizzle with Brown Sugar Barbecue Sauce (recipe follows).

BROWN SUGAR BARBECUE SAUCE

Pour cooking liquid from Instant Pot or slow cooker into a small saucepan over high heat. Boil for 10 to 12 minutes or until thickened and reduced by one third.

Sweet Heat
Roasted Ribs

Pulled Pork
With Brown Sugar
Barbecue Sauce

5 More Ideas for Pulled Pork

Sandwiches? Sure! But how about nachos, loaded baked potatoes and more...

1 BARBECUE NACHOS
Trade cooked pulled pork for ground beef in your favorite nachos recipe. Drizzle with barbecue sauce in addition to salsa.

2 LOADED POTATOES
Split open a baked potato and stir in butter, sour cream and salt, then top with warmed pulled pork and shredded cheddar cheese. Return to oven to melt the cheese, then top with chopped scallions.

3 PORK CARNITAS TACOS Toss pulled pork with a drizzle of oil, then broil for 3 to 5 minutes, turning occasionally, until thoroughly heated and beginning to crisp. Use as a filling for tacos, topped any way you like them.

4 FRIED RICE Chop pulled pork and use in place of beef or chicken in your favorite fried rice recipe.

5 EMPANADAS Roll and cut refrigerated pie dough into 3-inch circles. Place 1 to 2 tablespoons of pulled pork in each, fold, and crimp edges to seal. Bake at 350 F for 15 to 20 minutes or until golden brown. Serve with leftover barbecue sauce or sour cream.

Skillet Chicken & Fall Vegetable Potpie

This is a great use for rotisserie chicken. For an even faster version, substitute frozen biscuits. Simply place on top and bake as instructed.

EASY | FAMILY FAVORITE

TIME 50 minutes
(20 minutes active)

MAKES 6 servings

INGREDIENTS

- 2 tablespoons unsalted butter
- 1 medium Yukon Gold potato, cubed
- 2 small turnips, cubed
- 2 carrots, peeled and sliced into thin rounds
- 2 celery ribs, chopped
- 1 small onion, peeled and diced
- 2 cloves garlic, minced
- 1 cup frozen peas
- ¾ cup whole milk
- ¾ cup lower-sodium chicken stock
- 1 (10.5-ounce) can cream of chicken soup
- 2 cups cubed cooked chicken
- ½ teaspoon rubbed sage
- ½ teaspoon thyme
- ½ teaspoon kosher salt
- ¼ teaspoon ground black pepper

FOR BISCUITS

- 2 cups self-rising flour, plus more for dusting
- ¼ cup butter
- ¾ cup buttermilk
- 1 tablespoon unsalted butter, melted

1. Preheat oven to 425 F.

2. In a 12-inch cast-iron skillet over medium-high heat, melt butter. Saute potatoes and turnips for 5 to 7 minutes; add carrots, celery, onion and garlic, and saute 5 to 7 minutes more. Stir in peas.

3. In a large bowl, whisk together milk, stock and soup. Stir in chicken, sage, thyme, salt and pepper; pour into skillet. Reduce heat to simmer while you make the biscuits.

4. To make biscuits: In a mixing bowl, combine flour and butter with your hands or a pastry cutter until butter is roughly the size of peas. Stir in buttermilk until dough forms. Turn out onto a lightly floured surface and knead once or twice, then pat together into a disk. Roll or press into an 8-inch circle about 1 inch thick.

5. Using a 2-inch cookie cutter, cut out 8 biscuits, rerolling scraps as needed. Place biscuits on top of warm chicken mixture and brush with melted butter.

6. Bake for 20 to 25 minutes until biscuits are browned and chicken mixture is bubbling.

Bar-B-Cups

Canned biscuit dough and browned ground beef in barbecue sauce come together in this spin on sloppy Joes.

EASY | FAMILY FAVORITE | QUICK

TIME 30 minutes
(15 minutes active)

MAKES 10 biscuit cups

Skillet Chicken & Fall Vegetable Potpie

INGREDIENTS

- 2 teaspoons olive oil
- ½ medium red onion, diced
- 8 ounces lean ground beef
- 1 teaspoon kosher salt
- ½ teaspoon ground black pepper
- 2 cloves garlic, minced
- ½ cup barbecue sauce
- 1 (12-ounce) can refrigerated biscuits (such as Pillsbury)
- 2 tablespoons minced cilantro, for garnish

1. Preheat oven to 350 F.

2. In a skillet over medium-high heat, warm oil. Add onion and saute until softened, about 5 minutes. Add beef, salt and pepper, breaking up with a wooden spoon, and brown for 3 to 5 minutes. Add garlic and cook 1 minute more. Drain excess grease. Stir in barbecue sauce. Set aside.

3. Using your fingers, press biscuit dough into muffin tin holes to form cups. Place 2 tablespoons meat mixture into each cup. Bake for 12 to 15 minutes, or until biscuits are golden brown. Sprinkle with cilantro to serve.

Herb-Roasted Chicken Breasts & Grapes

Grapes are at their peak in fall, and they take on an even on sweeter flavor when roasted. Add a salad, and you've got dinner in less than an hour.

EASY | GLUTEN-FREE

TIME 1 hour (10 minutes active)

MAKES 4 servings

INGREDIENTS

- 4 bone-in chicken breasts
- 1 teaspoon salt
- ½ teaspoon ground black pepper
- 4 cloves garlic, peeled and minced
- 1 tablespoon fresh rosemary or thyme leaves, minced
- 2 tablespoons olive oil
- 4 small bunches of red grapes, about 1 cup each
- 1 lemon, quartered

1. Preheat oven to 350 F.

2. Pat chicken dry with paper towels and gently loosen the skin with your fingers. In a small bowl, stir together salt, pepper, garlic and rosemary.

3. Divide garlic mixture evenly between chicken pieces, spooning it beneath the skin and spreading it on top. Rub oil on chicken and place in a large oven-proof skillet. Tuck grapes and lemon between chicken and roast for 45 to 50 minutes or until a probe thermometer registers 165 F.

Herb-Roasted Chicken Breasts & Grapes

**Pomegranate-Glazed
Chicken Cutlets**

quick tip

To make your own quick-
cooking chicken cutlets,
pound two chicken
breasts with a mallet
to slightly flatten, then
cut in half lengthwise.

Pomegranate-Glazed Chicken Cutlets

Pair this North African-inspired dish with Brussels sprouts.

EASY | GLUTEN-FREE | QUICK
TIME 25 minutes
(10 minutes active)
MAKES 4 servings

INGREDIENTS

- 2 tablespoons olive oil, divided
- 4 boneless, skinless chicken cutlets
- 1 teaspoon kosher salt
- ½ teaspoon ground black pepper
- 2 tablespoons harissa spice (such as Mina)
- 1 cup pomegranate juice
- ½ cup pomegranate arils

1. In a large skillet over medium-high heat, warm oil. Season chicken with salt and pepper and brown 2 to 3 minutes per side, working in batches if needed.
2. Add harissa and pomegranate juice, reduce heat to medium-low and simmer, uncovered, for 10 minutes or until sauce is thickened and chicken is cooked through. Stir in pomegranate arils just before serving.

Pork Medallions in Mustard Sauce

The rich, creamy sauce comes together in less than 10 minutes.

EASY | FAMILY FAVORITE | GLUTEN-FREE
TIME 35 minutes
(10 minutes active)
MAKES 4 servings

INGREDIENTS

- 2 tablespoons olive oil, divided
- 1 (1½ -pound) pork tenderloin, cut at an angle into ½-inch-thick medallions
- 1 teaspoon kosher salt
- ½ teaspoon ground black pepper
- 1 small shallot, minced
- 1 clove garlic, minced
- ½ cup white wine
- 1½ tablespoons chopped fresh rosemary or tarragon, plus more for garnish
- 1 cup lower-sodium chicken broth
- ¾ cup heavy cream
- 2 teaspoons Dijon mustard

1. In a large skillet over medium-high heat, warm 1 tablespoon oil. Season pork with salt and pepper and brown 2 to 3 minutes per side, working in batches if needed. Remove from pan and cover to keep warm.
2. Add remaining oil to skillet. Add shallot and saute until softened, about 3 minutes; add garlic and cook 1 minute more. Add wine, rosemary, broth and cream, whisking to combine, and reduce heat to medium-low. Simmer until sauce is slightly thickened, about 5 to 8 minutes. Whisk in mustard. To serve, pour sauce over medallions and garnish with herbs.

Beet & Fennel Risotto

Bold color matches the flavor of this dish. Omit the goat cheese garnish for a vegan entree.

GLUTEN-FREE | SPECIAL OCCASION | VEGETARIAN
TIME 50 minutes (all active)
MAKES 4 servings

INGREDIENTS

- 2 medium red beets, raw, peeled
- 4 cups lower-sodium vegetable broth
- 2 tablespoons unsalted butter
- 2 tablespoons olive oil
- 1 small onion, finely chopped
- ½ small fennel bulb, finely chopped
- 1½ teaspoons kosher salt, divided
- 1 teaspoon freshly ground black pepper, divided
- 1 cup arborio rice
- 1 clove garlic, minced
- ½ cup white wine
- 2 ounces goat cheese, crumbled, for garnish
  Fresh parsley leaves, for garnish

1. Use a box grater to grate beets into a bowl. Set aside.
2. Pour broth into a microwave-safe liquid measuring cup and heat until hot, about 3 minutes; keep warm by microwaving for 30 seconds periodically throughout cooking.
3. In a large skillet over medium-high heat, warm butter and oil. Add onion and fennel and saute until softened, about 5 minutes. Add beets, 1 teaspoon salt and ½ teaspoon pepper and saute 5 to 8 minutes more. Add rice, garlic and wine and stir to combine; cook for 2 to 3 minutes.
4. Reduce heat to medium. Add 1 cup hot broth and remaining salt and pepper; stir constantly until absorbed. Repeat three more times, stirring constantly, until rice is al dente, about 30 minutes. Top individual servings with goat cheese and parsley.

---

quick tip

Beet juice can stain your skin, clothing and kitchen surfaces; consider wearing disposable gloves when handling.

---

quick tip

Spread ingredients in an even layer on the sheet pan—that way, they'll cook evenly.

**Shrimp Scampi With
Blistered Tomatoes, page 60**

chapter five

Sheet Pan Suppers

Perfect for busy weeknights, these time-saving meals come together in minutes. Even better, since there's only one pan, cleanup is a cinch.

Italian Sausage & Peppers

Roasting the sausages at a lower temperature helps prevent them from bursting.

EASY | FAMILY FAVORITE | GLUTEN-FREE
TIME 45 minutes
(10 minutes active)
MAKES 4 servings

INGREDIENTS

- 4   Italian sausages
- 1   half red onion, peeled and quartered
- 1   pound mini sweet peppers (such as Pero Family Farms), halved and seeded
- 1   bunch Broccolini
- 1   head red radicchio, quartered
- 2   tablespoons olive oil
- ½   teaspoon crushed red pepper flakes
- ½   teaspoon kosher salt
- ¼   teaspoon ground black pepper
- 2   cups marinara or pizza sauce

1. Preheat oven to 350 F.
2. Use the tip of a sharp knife to prick each sausage once or twice.
3. In a mixing bowl, toss vegetables with oil, red pepper flakes, salt and black pepper. Spread onion and mini peppers on a rimmed sheet pan (reserve Broccolini and radicchio); tuck sausage among them. Bake for 25 minutes.

quick tip

Add toasted rolls and mozzarella cheese to make Italian hoagies.

4. Remove pan from oven, turn sausages, peppers and onions, add Broccolini and radicchio and bake 10 minutes more. Serve sausages, onions and peppers with warmed marinara or pizza sauce for dipping; serve Broccolini and radicchio on the side.

Shrimp Scampi With Blistered Tomatoes

Serve with a spinach salad and a crusty baguette to soak up all the garlic oil.

QUICK | SPECIAL OCCASION
TIME 25 minutes (all active)
MAKES 4 servings

INGREDIENTS

- 2   (10-ounce) containers cherry or grape tomatoes
- 6   cloves garlic, smashed
- 1   lemon, sliced
- 3   tablespoons olive oil, divided
- ½   teaspoon dried basil, divided
- ½   teaspoon oregano, divided
- 1   teaspoon kosher salt, divided
- ½   teaspoon ground black pepper, divided
- 1½ pounds peeled and deveined raw shrimp

1. Preheat oven to 400 F.
2. In a mixing bowl, toss tomatoes, garlic and lemon with 1 tablespoon oil and half of each seasoning. Spread tomatoes on a rimmed sheet pan and bake for 8 to 10 minutes, shaking the pan once or twice.
3. In the same mixing bowl, toss shrimp with remaining oil and spices. Remove pan from oven; add shrimp and bake for 8 to 10 minutes more, shaking the pan once or twice. Remove garlic cloves before serving.

Italian Sausage & Peppers

5 Easy Stir-Together Sauces

Dress up any sheet pan dinner with one of these quick options.

❶ ARUGULA PESTO
Pulse 3 cups arugula leaves, ¼ cup walnuts and ½ teaspoon kosher salt in a food processor. With the machine on, pour ⅓ cup olive oil through the tube until the sauce is smooth. Stir in ½ cup grated Parmesan.

❷ SPICY MAYO Whisk together 1 cup mayonnaise with ¼ teaspoon smoked paprika and 2 tablespoons Sriracha sauce.

❸ LEMON-GARLIC AIOLI
Mash 2 garlic cloves into a paste with ¼ teaspoon kosher salt. Whisk together with 1 cup mayonnaise and zest and juice of half a lemon.

❹ CHIMICHURRI Whisk together 1 minced shallot, 3 minced garlic cloves, ½ seeded and minced jalapeño, ¼ cup red wine vinegar, ½ teaspoon kosher salt, ⅓ cup each finely chopped cilantro and parsley, 2 tablespoons finely chopped oregano and ¾ cup olive oil. (Sauce will not emulsify—that's OK.)

❺ GINGER-PEANUT Whisk together ½ cup creamy peanut butter, 2 tablespoons soy sauce, 1 tablespoon rice wine vinegar, 2 teaspoons Sriracha sauce, 1 tablespoon grated ginger, 2 teaspoons honey and ¼ cup warm water until smooth. If consistency is too thick, add more warm water to thin.

Salmon, Brussels Sprouts & Scallions With Yogurt-Dill Sauce

Salmon, Brussels Sprouts & Scallions With Yogurt-Dill Sauce

Dress up this simple dinner with a tangy yogurt-dill sauce.

EASY | FAMILY FAVORITE | GLUTEN-FREE
TIME 35 minutes
(10 minutes active)
MAKES 4 servings

INGREDIENTS

- 1½ pounds Brussels sprouts, halved
- 1 tablespoon olive oil
- 1 teaspoon kosher salt, divided
- ½ teaspoon ground black pepper, divided
- 4 (6-8 ounce) salmon fillets
- 1 bunch scallions, roots trimmed

1. Preheat oven to 425 F.
2. In a mixing bowl, toss Brussels sprouts with oil and season with half the salt and pepper. Place on a rimmed sheet pan, cut-side down, and bake for 10 to 12 minutes or until browned.
3. Remove pan from oven, flip the Brussels sprouts cut-side up; season salmon with remaining salt and pepper and add to the pan, along with scallions. Bake for 12 to 15 minutes or until salmon is cooked through. Serve with Yogurt-Dill Sauce (recipe follows).

YOGURT-DILL SAUCE
In a mixing bowl, whisk together 1 cup Greek yogurt; zest and juice of half a lemon, 1 tablespoon olive oil, 2 tablespoons chopped fresh dill, ½ teaspoon kosher salt and ¼ teaspoon ground black pepper.

Pork Chops, Carrots & Smashed Potatoes With Herb-Infused Oil

Herb oil is a great way to use a small amount of any fresh herbs that may be about to wilt.

EASY | GLUTEN-FREE | QUICK
TIME 35 minutes
(15 minutes active)
MAKES 4 servings

INGREDIENTS

- 1 tablespoon olive oil
- 4 bone-in pork chops
- 8-12 medium carrots, scrubbed
- ½ teaspoon kosher salt
- ¼ teaspoon ground black pepper
- 1½ pounds baby Yukon Gold potatoes

1. Preheat oven to 375 F. Drizzle rimmed sheet pan with oil. Place pork chops and carrots on pan; season with salt and pepper and bake for 20 minutes.
2. Meanwhile, in a large saucepan, add potatoes and enough water to cover them by 1 inch. Bring to a boil over high heat and simmer for 15 to 20 minutes or until soft. Drain and, while warm, smash each with a spatula so that it remains mostly whole and is about ½ inch thick.
3. Remove pan from oven. Add smashed potatoes and drizzle each with 1 to 2 teaspoons of Herb-Infused Oil (recipe follows). Drizzle pork and carrots, too. Return pan to oven, and bake for 10 minutes more to brown potatoes.

HERB-INFUSED OIL
In a small saucepan over low heat, add ⅓ cup olive oil. Stir in 1 minced clove of garlic, half a minced shallot, ½ teaspoon each crushed red pepper flakes, kosher salt and ground black pepper and 1 tablespoon each chopped parsley, sage, chives or other herbs. Warm for 5 to 10 minutes.

Halibut in Parchment Packets

As the packets bake, the flavor of lemon and caper infuses both the fish and the carrots.

EASY | GLUTEN-FREE | QUICK
TIME 20 minutes
(5 minutes active)
MAKES 4 servings

INGREDIENTS

- 4 (8-ounce) halibut fillets
- ½ teaspoon kosher salt
- ½ teaspoon ground black pepper
- 2 cups matchstick carrots, divided
- ¼ cup olive oil, divided
- 1 lemon, sliced into 8 rounds
- ¼ cup drained capers, divided
- 4 sprigs fresh thyme

1. Preheat oven to 400 F.
2. Cut four 12x16-inch sheets of parchment. Fold each in half vertically, then cut so that when sheet is unfolded, it will be heart-shaped. Sprinkle fish with salt and pepper.
3. Divide ingredients evenly between parchment sheets and stacking them to the right of the fold, starting with carrots, then fish, oil, lemon slices, capers and thyme. Fold left half of paper over top and then make small folds, like pleats around the rim, to seal and form packets.
4. Place packets on a rimmed sheet pan and bake for 15 minutes. Serve with rice.

Pesto Chicken Breasts With Kale & Potatoes

Juice from the roasted lemons helps brighten all the flavors of this complete meal.

EASY | FAMILY FAVORITE

TIME 1 hour (20 minutes active)

MAKES 4 servings

INGREDIENTS

½ cup jarred pesto, divided

¼ cup olive oil, divided

2½ teaspoons kosher salt, divided

1 teaspoon ground black pepper, divided

1 pound baby Yukon Gold potatoes, halved

4 boneless, skinless chicken breasts

6 cups curly kale leaves, stemmed and chopped

2 lemons, halved

1. Preheat oven to 425 F.
2. In a mixing bowl, stir half the pesto, 2 tablespoons oil, 1 teaspoon salt and ½ teaspoon pepper; add potatoes and toss. Place potatoes on a rimmed sheet pan and bake for 10 to 12 minutes.
3. Meanwhile, in the same mixing bowl, add remaining pesto, 1 tablespoon oil, 1 teaspoon salt, and remaining pepper. Toss in chicken. Remove sheet pan from oven and add chicken to pan. Bake for 25 to 30 minutes.
4. In a clean mixing bowl, add kale, remaining oil and remaining salt. Remove sheet pan from oven and tuck kale leaves among chicken and potatoes. Add lemon halves to pan. Bake for 10 minutes more, or until kale is beginning to brown and chicken registers 165 F on a probe thermometer. Squeeze roasted lemons over pan before serving.

Cumin Chicken Thighs & Peppers

Moist and tender chicken thighs are a forgiving cut; it's hard to overcook them, even under the broiler.

EASY | FAMILY FAVORITE | QUICK

TIME 20 minutes (5 minutes active)

MAKES 4 servings

INGREDIENTS

¼ cup olive oil

2 teaspoons cumin

1 teaspoon smoked paprika

1 teaspoon kosher salt

¼ teaspoon ground black pepper

2 red bell peppers, seeded and sliced into strips

1 poblano pepper, chopped

1 Cubanelle or Hungarian wax pepper, sliced into rings (seeds removed)

1 red onion, sliced vertically

2 cloves garlic, minced

5-6 boneless, skinless chicken thighs, chopped into bite-sized pieces
Hummus, for serving
Toasted pita bread, for serving

1. Preheat broiler.
2. In a small bowl, whisk together oil and spices. In a medium bowl, add peppers, onion and garlic. Toss with half the oil mixture. Place on a rimmed sheet pan. In the same bowl, toss chicken and remaining oil mixture. Add to sheet pan in a single layer.
3. Broil for 8 to 12 minutes, shaking the pan and turning the chicken and vegetables several times with a spatula to ensure even cooking.
4. To serve, spread ⅓ cup hummus in four shallow bowls and top with chicken and vegetables; serve with pita.

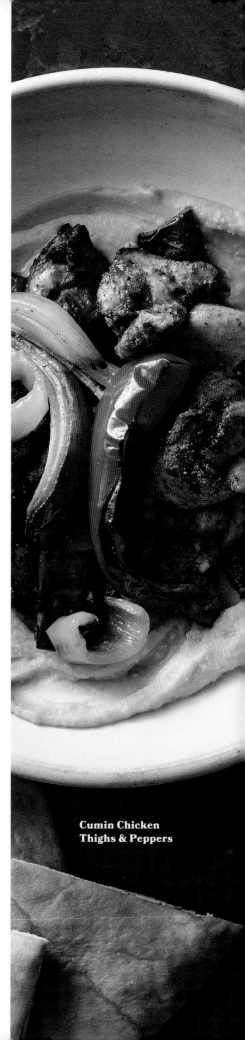

Cumin Chicken Thighs & Peppers

Secrets to Sheet Pan Success

The convenience of a one-pan meal is hard to beat. Try these tips to amp up your recipe results.

1 START WITH A STURDY PAN The materials and quality used to make a 13x18-inch sheet pan can vary. Thin pans may warp in the oven's high heat, causing ingredients to shift and sauces to pool. Invest in a heavy aluminum pan.

2 IT'S ALL IN THE TIMING Begin with slower-cooking ingredients, then add quicker-cooking ones after the first items have softened and caramelized. In general, hearty root vegetables, such as carrots and potatoes, will need longer cook times than tender items, like green beans or peppers. Similarly, bone-in chicken will need more cook time than delicate fish fillets.

3 TWO PANS MAY BE BETTER THAN ONE If you're concerned about overfilling a sheet pan or are following a recipe that works in stages, divide the recipe's ingredients between two pans.

4 ADD A FINISHING TOUCH For an extra layer of caramelization and browning, consider cranking up the broiler for the few final minutes of cooking. Just keep a close eye on the food to avoid burning.

Pasta
Bolognese,
page 68

quick tip

Toss the sauce with
the cooked pasta
before serving so it
coats each strand.

chapter six

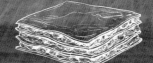

Pasta, Pizzas & Sandwiches

These family-favorite dishes are great for
fall game-day gatherings, but they're just as
enjoyable on ordinary weeknights, too.

PASTA, PIZZAS & SANDWICHES

Pasta Bolognese

The goal with this recipe is to cook the meat until it is completely dry for maximum flavor, then rehydrate it with wine, milk and chopped tomatoes.

FAMILY FAVORITE | SPECIAL OCCASION
TIME 2 hours, 10 minutes
(45 minutes active)
MAKES 6 to 8 servings

INGREDIENTS

- 2 tablespoons olive oil, divided
- 1¼ pounds ground chuck
- 1 pound ground pork
- ¼ pound pancetta, diced
- 1 onion, diced
- 3 carrots, peeled and diced
- 2 celery stalks, diced
- 3 cloves garlic, minced
- 3 bay leaves
- ½ teaspoon dried basil
- ⅛ teaspoon cinnamon
  Pinch cayenne pepper
- 1 teaspoon kosher salt
- ½ teaspoon ground black pepper
- 1 cup red wine
- 2 cups whole milk
- 2 (28-ounce) cans chopped tomatoes, drained
- 1 tablespoon tomato paste
- 1 pound uncooked tagliatelle or fettuccine pasta
  Grated Parmesan cheese, for garnish
  Chopped fresh parsley, for garnish

1. In a large Dutch oven over medium heat, warm 1 tablespoon oil. Add beef, pork and pancetta, and press into the bottom of the pan to fully brown, about 12 to 15 minutes. Stir and repeat for another 12 to 15 minutes until nearly all of the liquid is evaporated. Remove meat from Dutch oven; set aside.
2. Warm remaining oil in same Dutch oven; add onion, carrots, celery and garlic and saute, stirring often, until vegetables are softened, about 8 to 10 minutes. Return meat to pan. Add bay leaves, basil, cinnamon, cayenne, salt, pepper and wine, scraping up any browned bits from the bottom of the pan; cook for 5 minutes.
3. Stir in milk, tomatoes and tomato paste; reduce heat and simmer for 1 hour.
4. Cook pasta according to package directions. Toss pasta with sauce and garnish with Parmesan and parsley to serve.

Deep-Dish Pepperoni Pizza

Homemade dough, made with a bit of cornmeal for snap, is the key to this deep-dish pizza; store-bought dough just won't give you the same rise and texture.

FAMILY FAVORITE | SPECIAL OCCASION
TIME 3 hours, 15 minutes
(20 minutes active)
MAKES 1 pizza

INGREDIENTS

FOR DOUGH
- 1¾ cups all-purpose flour
- ¼ cup fine-ground cornmeal
- ¾ teaspoon salt
- ½ teaspoon powdered garlic
- ½ teaspoon instant yeast
- ¾ cup lukewarm water
- 1 tablespoon olive oil, plus more for oiling pan

FOR TOPPINGS
- 1¼ cup shredded mozzarella cheese, divided
- ½ cup pizza sauce
- 24 slices pepperoni

1. In a large mixing bowl, add all dough ingredients. Stir together to make a shaggy dough. Cover, let dough rest for 5 minutes, then repeat the following stretch-and-fold technique four times, with a 5-minute covered rest between each: With a dough scraper to gather up one side of the dough, stretch it and fold it over the top, give the bowl a quarter-turn and repeat three more times. Cover and let dough rest for 30 minutes.
2. In a 10-inch cast-iron skillet, pour an additional 1 tablespoon oil, swirling to coat the sides. Place dough in skillet, turning to coat. With fingertips, dimple and stretch the dough to completely fill the skillet. Cover and let dough rise for 2 hours.
3. Preheat oven to 450 F.
4. Cover dough with ¾ cup cheese, leaving a ½-inch border. Spoon sauce on top of cheese. Add pepperoni. Top with remaining cheese. Bake for 20 minutes until cheese is bubbly and beginning to brown.

Deep-Dish Mushroom Pizza With Fall Greens Pesto

Try this dish with Taleggio—a semi-soft Italian cheese similar to brie—in place of the mozzarella for even richer flavor.

SPECIAL OCCASION | VEGETARIAN
TIME 3 hours, 30 minutes
(20 minutes active)
MAKES 1 pizza

INGREDIENTS

FOR DOUGH
- 1¾ cups all-purpose flour
- ¼ cup fine-ground cornmeal
- ¾ teaspoon salt
- ½ teaspoon powdered garlic
- ½ teaspoon instant yeast
- ¾ cup lukewarm water
- 1 tablespoon olive oil, plus more for pan

FOR TOPPINGS
- 6 ounces mixed gourmet mushrooms
- 1 tablespoon butter

68 FLAVORS OF FALL

quick tip

For a make-ahead approach to this pizza, refrigerate the dough after its first rise for up to 2 days.

Deep-Dish Pepperoni Pizza

1¼ cups shredded mozzarella cheese, divided

½ cup Fall Greens Pesto (recipe follows)

1. In a large mixing bowl, add all dough ingredients. Stir together to make a shaggy dough. Cover, let dough rest for 5 minutes, then repeat the following stretch-and-fold technique four times, with a 5-minute covered rest between each: With a dough scraper to gather up one side of the dough, stretch it and fold it over the top, give the bowl a quarter-turn and repeat three more times. Cover and let dough rest for 30 minutes.

2. In a 10-inch cast-iron skillet, pour an additional 1 tablespoon oil, swirling to coat the sides. Place dough in skillet, turning to coat. With fingertips, dimple and stretch the dough to completely fill the skillet. Cover and let dough rise for 2 hours.

3. In a large skillet over medium heat, melt butter. Add mushrooms and saute, stirring often, until mushrooms have released most of their liquid, about 8 to 10 minutes. Set aside.

4. Preheat oven to 450 F.

5. Cover dough with ¾ cup cheese, leaving a ½-inch border. Spoon pesto on top of cheese. Add mushrooms. Top with remaining cheese. Bake for 20 minutes until cheese is bubbly and beginning to brown.

FALL GREENS PESTO

In the bowl of a food processor, combine ¼ cup toasted pine nuts, 2 garlic cloves, zest and juice of half a lemon, 4 cups chopped fresh collard, mustard or Swiss chard greens, ½ teaspoon kosher salt and ¼ teaspoon ground black pepper; pulse to combine. Then, with the motor running, pour 1 cup olive oil through the tube until mixture emulsifies. Stir in ½ cup grated Parmesan cheese.

Bratwurst, Apple and Cabbage Hoagies

The nutmeg flavor of bratwurst, an upper-Midwestern favorite, pairs perfectly with sauteed apples and cabbage.

EASY | FAMILY FAVORITE

TIME 30 minutes
(5 minutes active)

MAKES 4 servings

INGREDIENTS

- 4 bratwurst
- ½ small head of green cabbage, cut in ¼- ½-inch thick slices
- 2 apples, cored and sliced
- 3 tablespoons unsalted butter, melted
- ½ teaspoon kosher salt
- ¼ teaspoon ground black pepper
- 4 hoagie rolls
  Spicy brown mustard, optional

1. Preheat oven to 350 F.
2. Place the bratwurst on a rimmed baking sheet and bake for 10 minutes on middle rack.
3. Meanwhile, in a mixing bowl, lightly toss cabbage and apple with butter, salt and pepper.
4. Place cabbage and apple mixture on pan alongside sausages. Bake for 10 to 15 minutes, turning cabbage and sausages once during cooking.
5. Turn broiler to high, and broil for 2 to 3 minutes to brown.
6. Divide cabbage between rolls, top with apples and sausages; serve with mustard, if desired.

Kentucky Hot Browns

This hearty open-faced sandwich was born at Louisville, Kentucky's Brown Hotel in the 1920s.

FAMILY FAVORITE | QUICK

TIME 20 minutes
(15 active)

MAKES 4 servings

INGREDIENTS

- 2 tablespoons unsalted butter
- 2 tablespoons all-purpose flour
- 2 cups whole milk
- 2 cups shredded white cheddar cheese
- ¼ cup grated Parmesan cheese, plus more for sprinkling
- ½ teaspoon kosher salt
- ¼ teaspoon ground black pepper
- 1/8 teaspoon nutmeg
- 4 (1-inch-thick) slices artisan bread, lightly toasted
- 1 pound sliced turkey
- 2 tomatoes, sliced
- 6-8 strips bacon, cooked
  Chives, for garnish

1. Preheat broiler.

2. In a saucepan over medium-low heat, melt butter. Whisk in flour to make a roux; cook for 2 minutes, stirring, until fully combined. Slowly whisk in milk; raise heat to medium-high and bring to a boil. Cook, whisking, until thickened, about 5 minutes. Remove from heat; add cheeses, salt, pepper and nutmeg, stirring to melt. Set aside.

3. Arrange toasted bread on a rimmed baking sheet. Top each slice with turkey and tomato. Spoon cheese sauce over each. Broil until cheese is melted and bubbly, about 2 to 3 minutes. Top each sandwich with 1 or 2 strips of bacon and sprinkle with chives to serve.

quick tip

Toasting the bread before assembling helps support the melty, cheesy sauce.

Short Rib Ragù

If using a slow cooker, brown ribs in a skillet, deglaze with wine and pour into the slow cooker, then continue with the recipe.

EASY | MAKE AHEAD
TIME 8 hours for slow cooker, 1 hour for Instant Pot (30 minutes active)
MAKES 4 servings

INGREDIENTS

- 2 tablespoons olive oil, divided
- 2 pounds short ribs (4 to 6 ribs)
- 1 teaspoon kosher salt, divided
- ½ teaspoon ground black pepper, divided
- 1 onion, diced
- 2 cloves garlic, minced
- ½ cup red wine
- 1 (28-ounce) can crushed tomatoes
- ½ teaspoon dried oregano
- ½ teaspoon dried basil

1. In a large skillet heated up over medium-high heat (or the inner pot of an Instant Pot set to saute), warm 1 tablespoon oil; season ribs with ½ teaspoon salt and ¼ teaspoon pepper and brown on all sides (about 2 to 3 minutes per side). Remove the ribs and set aside.
2. Add remaining oil and saute onion and garlic until softened, about 5 to 7 minutes. Deglaze with wine, scraping up any browned bits from the bottom of the pan, about 1 to 2 minutes. Stir in tomatoes with their juices, oregano, basil and remaining salt and pepper.
3. If using a slow cooker, add mixture to pot, stir, cover and set on low for 8 hours. If using an Instant Pot, add ½ cup water, stir, cover and set to 40 minutes on high, sealed. Allow pressure to release naturally.
4. Remove meat and bones, trim any large pieces of fat or membrane and discard along with bones. Shred meat with two forks or chop and return to pot, stirring to combine. Serve with pasta.

Smash-Style Double Patty Melts

Smashing the patties flat on a hot griddle cooks them quickly, and provides edges with lots of deliciously crispy browned bits.

EASY | FAMILY FAVORITE | QUICK
TIME 30 minutes (all active)
MAKES 4 servings

INGREDIENTS

- 2 tablespoons unsalted butter
- 1 red onion, peeled and chopped
- 2 tablespoons canola or vegetable oil
- 2 pounds ground chuck
- 1 teaspoon kosher salt
- ½ teaspoon ground black pepper
- 4 slices Swiss cheese
- 8 pieces of rye sandwich bread, toasted

1. On a large cast-iron griddle or flat skillet over medium heat, melt butter. Add onions and saute, stirring occasionally, until softened and beginning to caramelize, about 15 to 20 minutes. Remove and set aside.
2. Holding a paper towel with tongs, wipe out the griddle. Add oil and set heat to medium-high. Divide beef into 8 equal portions, rolling each into a loose ball. Place balls onto griddle, two or four at a time depending on size, and smash them flat with a spatula. Season with salt and pepper.
3. Cook for 2 minutes, then flip; top each with a spoonful of onions and a slice of cheese. Cook 1 minute more, until cheese begins to melt. Remove from pan and set aside. (You will need 4 patties cooked this way.)
4. For the remaining patties, cook for 2 minutes, flip and cook 1 minute more. Place the second patties on top of the first (so the onion and cheese are sandwiched between both patties), then place patties on toasted bread and top with remaining bread.

Buttery Old Bay Shrimp Rolls

Dripping with melted butter, these warm shrimp rolls put a cool-weather spin on the summertime favorite dish.

EASY | FAMILY FAVORITE | QUICK
TIME 10 minutes (all active)
MAKES 4 servings

INGREDIENTS

- 1½ pounds peeled and deveined raw shrimp
- 1 tablespoon olive oil
- 2 teaspoons Old Bay seasoning
- ¼ teaspoon kosher salt
- ½ cup unsalted butter
- 4 top-split hot dog or lobster rolls
- 8 leaves butter lettuce
- 1 tablespoon minced chives, for garnish

1. Preheat oven to 400 F.
2. In a medium bowl, toss shrimp, oil, Old Bay seasoning and salt. Spread in an even layer on a rimmed baking sheet. Roast for 8 to 10 minutes.
3. In a microwave-safe bowl, add butter and microwave for 30 seconds to melt; toss with warm shrimp.
4. To serve, line each roll with 2 lettuce leaves, then top with shrimp and sprinkle with chives to garnish.

Start With a Flatbread...

Then jazz it up with any one of these creative topping combinations.

---

① BARBECUE CHICKEN
Spread flatbread with ⅓ to ½ cup bottled barbecue sauce; top with 1 cup chopped cooked chicken, 1 chopped scallion and ⅔ to ¾ cup shredded cheddar. Bake 10 to 12 minutes at 425 F.

② JALAPEÑO & PINEAPPLE Spread flatbread with ⅓ to ½ cup salsa; top with 3 strips cooked and crumbled bacon, ½ cup pineapple chunks, ½ a sliced jalapeño and ⅔ to ¾ cup shredded mozzarella. Bake 10 to 12 minutes at 425 F.

③ SUN-DRIED TOMATO & SALMON Spread flatbread with ⅓ to ½ cup sun-dried tomato pesto; top with 1 to 2 ounces chopped smoked salmon and 1 to 2 ounces crumbled goat cheese. Bake 10 to 12 minutes at 425 F. Garnish with drained capers, thinly sliced red onion and fresh dill.

④ BROCCOLI & CHEESE
Spread flatbread with ⅓ to ½ cup ricotta cheese; top with 1 cup steamed broccoli florets, ½ cup chopped ham and ⅔ to ¾ cup shredded cheddar. Bake 10 to 12 minutes at 425 F. Garnish with red pepper flakes.

⑤ FIG & BLUE CHEESE
Spread flatbread with ⅓ to ½ cup fig preserves; top with 2 to 3 slices of prosciutto and ⅓ to ½ cup blue cheese crumbles. Bake 10 to 12 minutes at 425 F. Garnish with fresh parsley.

Cheesy Baked Macaroni & Butternut Squash

Amp up the nutrition and flavor with cut-up butternut squash.

———

FAMILY FAVORITE | VEGETARIAN

TIME 1 hour, 20 minutes
(25 minutes active)

MAKES 6 to 8 servings

INGREDIENTS

   Cooking spray
3 cups cubed, peeled butternut squash
1 cup vegetable stock
1½ cups whole milk
2 cloves garlic, minced
1 pound shell or elbow pasta
1½ teaspoons kosher salt
½ teaspoon freshly ground black pepper
¼ teaspoon nutmeg
1½ cups grated Gruyere cheese
1 cup grated cheddar cheese
¼ cup grated Parmesan cheese, divided
3 teaspoons olive oil
¾ cup panko breadcrumbs
   Parsley, for garnish

1. Preheat oven to 375 F. Coat a 9x13-inch baking dish with cooking spray.
2. In a large Dutch oven over high heat, stir squash, stock, milk and garlic and bring to a boil. Reduce heat and simmer for 20 to 30 minutes or until the squash is tender.
3. Meanwhile, cook pasta according to package directions; drain and set aside.
4. Using an immersion blender, puree squash mixture (alternately, ladle into a blender and puree in small batches, leaving the top vented and wrapped in a kitchen towel). Add salt, pepper, nutmeg, Gruyere, cheddar and 2 tablespoons Parmesan and stir to melt. Add in the pasta and stir to combine. Pour mixture into baking dish.
5. To make topping, in a skillet over medium heat, warm oil; add breadcrumbs, stirring often, until browned, about 3 minutes. Stir in remaining Parmesan and sprinkle evenly over prepared dish. Bake for 20 to 25 minutes or until bubbly and browned. Garnish with parsley to serve.

Chicken Salad Sandwiches With Grapes & Pecans

Mixing the chicken with cream cheese makes it easy to spread.

———

EASY | QUICK

TIME 10 minutes (all active)

MAKES 4 to 6 servings

INGREDIENTS

3 tablespoons cream cheese, softened
3 tablespoons mayonnaise
1 teaspoon honey
1 teaspoon kosher salt
½ teaspoon ground black pepper
1 tablespoon fresh dill, chopped
   Pinch of smoked paprika
2 chicken breasts, cooked, cooled and cubed
¼ cup toasted, chopped pecans
½ cup grapes, halved

1. In the bowl of a food processor, add cream cheese, mayonnaise, honey, salt, pepper, dill and paprika; pulse to blend. Add chicken and pulse to chop and blend (about 8 to 10 times). Add pecans and pulse 1 to 2 times to combine.
2. Remove from processor and place in a mixing bowl; fold in grapes. Serve on toast or bread with lettuce and mayonnaise.

Chicken Salad Sandwiches With Grapes & Pecans

Cheesy Baked Macaroni & Butternut Squash

quick tip

Cooking butternut squash in the milk mixture infuses this spin on macaroni and cheese with fall favor.

Chili Mac

Easy, cheesy and
crowd-pleasing.

———

FAMILY FAVORITE | QUICK
TIME 25 minutes (all active)
MAKES 6 to 8 servings

INGREDIENTS

1 tablespoon olive oil
1 medium yellow
   onion, diced
8 ounces lean
   ground beef
2 teaspoons kosher salt,
   divided
2 cloves garlic, minced
2 teaspoons
   chili powder
1 teaspoon cumin
½ teaspoon
   dried oregano
½ teaspoon ground
   black pepper
1 (28-ounce) can
   crushed tomatoes
2 cups lower-sodium
   beef broth
1 (15-ounce) can kidney
   beans, drained and
   rinsed
2 cups elbow pasta

½ cup half-and-half
1½ cups shredded
    cheddar or pepper
    jack cheese, plus
    extra for garnish
2 scallions, sliced,
   for garnish

1. In a large Dutch oven
over medium-high heat,
warm oil. Add onion and
saute until softened, about
5 minutes. Add beef and
1 teaspoon salt, breaking
up with a wooden spoon,
and brown for 3 minutes.

2. Stir in chili powder,
cumin, oregano and
remaining salt and pepper.
Add tomatoes, broth,
beans and pasta, stirring
to combine.

3. Raise heat to high
and bring to a boil,
then reduce to simmer,
stirring occasionally, until
pasta is cooked, about
12 minutes.

4. Stir in half-and-half
and cheese. Top with
shredded cheese and
scallions to serve.

Pepperoni Sausage Pizza Pinwheels

If you sub a ready-made pizza dough ball for frozen bread dough, your pinwheels will be extra puffy.

FAMILY FAVORITE | SPECIAL OCCASION
TIME 1 hour, 30 minutes
(20 minutes active)
MAKES 4 to 6 servings

INGREDIENTS

- 1 (1-pound) frozen bread dough loaf, defrosted
- ½ cup pizza sauce, plus more for dipping
- 1 cup shredded mozzarella cheese, divided
- ¼ cup grated Parmesan cheese
- ¼ cup sliced pepperoni
- ¼ cup hot Italian sausage, cooked and crumbled
- 2 tablespoons chopped red onion
- ¼ teaspoon dried oregano
- ¼ teaspoon dried basil
- 2 tablespoons minced fresh basil, plus more for garnish
- ½ teaspoon crushed red pepper flakes, plus more for garnish

1. On a lightly floured surface, roll dough into a 18x12-inch rectangle. Spread sauce to within ½ inch of edges. Sprinkle with ½ cup mozzarella, Parmesan, pepperoni, sausage, onion and dried spices.
2. Roll up jelly-roll style, starting with a long side; pinch seam and ends to seal. (If you have time, wrap the log in plastic wrap and refrigerate for 30 minutes.)
3. Cut log into 7 to 9 slices, depending on thickness. Place tightly in a 10-inch cast-iron skillet. Cover skillet with a kitchen towel and let dough rise 30 to 40 minutes. Preheat oven to 400 F.
4. Bake 20 minutes. Sprinkle with remaining mozzarella and bake 10 minutes more.
5. Garnish with basil and pepper flakes to serve, with additional warmed pizza sauce on the side for dipping.

Spicy Shrimp, Tomato and Feta Pizza

Clams are popular on pizza, so why not shrimp? White shrimp harvest hits its peak in October.

EASY | FAMILY FAVORITE | QUICK
TIME 25 minutes
(10 minutes active)
MAKES 1 pizza

INGREDIENTS

- 1 (1-pound) purchased pizza dough ball or rolled 12-inch circle
- 1 cup ricotta cheese
- ¼ cup jarred sun-dried tomatoes, drained and chopped
- 1 tablespoon tomato paste
- 4 ounces peeled, deveined shrimp, with tails removed
- ½ teaspoon kosher salt
- ¼ teaspoon ground black pepper
- ½ teaspoon dried oregano
- ¼ teaspoon red pepper flakes, plus more for garnish
- ½ cup shredded mozzarella cheese
- ½ cup crumbled feta cheese Fresh basil, for garnish

1. Preheat oven to 450 F. Place a sheet pan or pizza baking stone in oven to heat.
2. Roll dough into a 12-inch circle or oval. In a bowl, stir together ricotta, tomatoes and tomato paste; spread evenly on dough.
3. Top shrimp, salt, pepper, oregano and pepper flakes; top with mozzarella and feta.
4. Bake 12 to 15 minutes or until cheese is bubbly and browned. Garnish with pepper flakes and basil to serve.

Chicken & Spinach White Pizza

Look for ready-made pizza dough—as a ball or as a pre-rolled circle—in your grocery store's bakery section.

EASY | FAMILY FAVORITE
TIME 25 minutes
(10 minutes active)
MAKES 1 pizza

INGREDIENTS

- 1 (1-pound) purchased pizza dough ball or rolled 12-inch circle
- 1 cup ricotta cheese
- ½ cup frozen chopped spinach, defrosted and drained
- 2 tablespoons jarred pesto
- ½ teaspoon salt
- ½ teaspoon ground black pepper
- 1 cup cooked chicken breast, cubed
- ¼ teaspoon red pepper flakes, plus more for garnish
- 1 cup shredded mozzarella cheese
- ¼ cup grated Parmesan cheese Fresh basil, for garnish

1. Preheat oven to 450 F. Place a sheet pan or pizza baking stone in oven to heat.
2. Roll dough into a 12-inch circle or oval. In a bowl, stir together ricotta, spinach and pesto; spread evenly on dough.
3. Sprinkle with salt, pepper and pepper flakes; top with chicken, mozzarella and Parmesan.
4. Bake 12 to 15 minutes or until cheese is bubbly and browned. Garnish with pepper flakes and basil to serve.

Cornbread Taco
Pie Casserole,
page 80

quick tip
To make this recipe even
easier, substitute two
1-ounce packets of taco
seasoning for the spices.

chapter seven

Casseroles

Whether they're meat-and-potatoes
mains or elegant, streusel-topped side dishes,
all kinds of delicious goodness awaits
beneath these browned, bubbly toppings.

Cornbread Taco Pie Casserole

Just add a salad to complete this hearty all-in-one meal.

EASY | FAMILY FAVORITE
TIME 1 hour, 10 minutes (20 minutes active)
MAKES 12 to 16 servings

INGREDIENTS
  Cooking spray
- 1 tablespoon canola oil
- 2 pounds lean ground beef
- 1 tablespoon chili powder
- 2 teaspoons cumin
- 1 teaspoon onion powder
- 1 teaspoon dried oregano
- 1 teaspoon kosher salt
- ½ teaspoon ground black pepper
- 2 (14-16-ounce) cans chopped tomatoes, drained
- 1 (4-ounce) can mild green chiles
- 2 (8.5-ounce) boxes corn muffin mix (such as Jiffy)
- 2 eggs, beaten
- ⅔ cups buttermilk
- 1 cup frozen corn kernels
- 1 cup sour cream, plus more for garnish
- 1 cup crumbled corn chips, divided
- 1½ cups shredded cheddar cheese, divided
- 1 tomato, chopped, for garnish
  Fresh cilantro, for garnish

1. Preheat oven to 400 F. Coat a 9x13-inch baking dish with cooking spray.
2. In a large skillet over medium-high heat, warm oil. Add beef and brown, breaking up with a spoon, for 8 to 10 minutes. Drain grease; stir in spices, tomatoes and chiles with their juices. Set aside.
3. In a mixing bowl, stir together muffin mix, eggs, buttermilk and corn. Pour half of batter into baking dish. Spoon half of beef mixture into center, leaving a 1-inch border.
4. Spread sour cream on top of beef mixture, top with half of corn chips and ½ cup cheese, then add the remaining beef mixture. Spoon remaining batter around the edges of beef mixture. Top with remaining corn chips and ½ cup cheese.
5. Bake for 40 to 45 minutes or until cornbread is puffed and golden brown. Top with remaining ½ cup cheese and bake 3 to 5 minutes more. Garnish with tomatoes and cilantro; serve with dollops of sour cream.

Green Bean & Brussels Sprouts Casserole

Two fall favorites—creamy green bean casserole and Brussels sprouts with bacon—combine in one powerhouse side.

FAMILY FAVORITE | SPECIAL OCCASION
TIME 1 hour, 10 minutes (40 minutes active)
MAKES 8 to 10 servings

INGREDIENTS
  Cooking spray
- 6 bacon strips
- 1 pound green beans, trimmed
- 1 pound trimmed and quartered fresh Brussels sprouts
- ½ cup butter, divided
- 1 (8-ounce) package sliced mushrooms, chopped
- 1 large shallot, chopped
- 6 tablespoons all-purpose flour
- 4 cups whole milk
- 1½ cups grated Parmesan cheese
- 2 teaspoons kosher salt
- ½ teaspoon ground black pepper
- ½ cup pecans, diced
- 1 cup crispy fried onions or shallots

quick tip
To keep vegetables bright green, blanch for 30 seconds in boiling water, then chill in an ice bath before sauteing.

1. Preheat oven to 350 F. Coat a 9x13-inch baking dish with cooking spray.
2. In a Dutch oven over medium heat, cook bacon until crisp, about 6 to 8 minutes. Drain bacon on paper towels; set aside. Reserve drippings in Dutch oven. Add green beans and Brussels sprouts to Dutch oven and saute until tender, about 8 to 10 minutes. Remove vegetables from Dutch oven.
3. Add 2 tablespoons butter to Dutch oven and raise heat to medium-high. Add mushrooms and shallot, and saute until softened, about 8 to 10 minutes. Transfer mushroom mixture to a small bowl.
4. Add remaining butter to Dutch oven; melt. Whisk in flour for 1 to 2 minutes. Gradually add milk, whisking constantly until smooth. Cook, whisking constantly, until thickened, about 4 minutes. Remove from heat, and whisk in Parmesan, salt and pepper until melted and smooth. Stir in pecans, reserved Brussels sprouts and green beans, and reserved mushroom mixture; spoon into baking dish.
5. Bake for 15 minutes. Meanwhile, crumble bacon.
6. Remove dish from oven; sprinkle crumbled bacon and fried onions or shallots over top. Return to oven and bake until bubbly, about 15 minutes.

Fall-Vegetable Shepherd's Pie

Shepherd's pie is a great way to use up leftover mashed potatoes. None on hand? Sub ready-made ones, available at most grocers.

GLUTEN-FREE | VEGETARIAN

TIME 1 hour, 10 minutes (15 minutes active)

MAKES 8 servings

INGREDIENTS

- 2 tablespoons extra-virgin olive oil
- 1 onion, diced
- 2 carrots, peeled and chopped
- 2 celery stalks, thinly sliced
- 1 cup cubed butternut squash
- 1 (8-ounce) package sliced mushrooms
- 2 garlic cloves, minced
- 2 teaspoons fresh thyme leaves
- 1 tablespoon tomato paste
- 1 bay leaf
- 1 teaspoon kosher salt
- ¼ teaspoon ground black pepper
- 1 cup French green lentils
- 4 cups vegetable broth
- 1 cup frozen peas
- 3-4 cups Ultimate Garlic Mashed Potatoes (see page 90)

1. Preheat oven to 400 F.

2. In a large Dutch oven over medium heat, warm oil. Add onion, carrots, celery, squash and mushrooms; saute until softened, about 8 to 10 minutes. Add garlic and cook 1 minute more.

3. Add thyme, tomato paste, bay leaf, salt, pepper, lentils and broth. Raise heat to bring to boil, then reduce to simmer, about 20 to 30 minutes or until lentils and squash are tender. Stir in peas.

4. Pour vegetable mixture into a 2-quart baking dish. Spread potatoes over top. Bake for 20 minutes or until bubbly.

Green Bean & Brussels Sprouts Casserole

quick tip

For extra crunch, look for panko breadcrumbs, which are drier and flakier than traditional packaged breadcrumbs.

Cheesy Cauliflower-Broccoli Casserole

Tater Tot-Topped Cowboy Casserole

Spiced meat and potatoes, all in one easy dish.

EASY | FAMILY FAVORITE | GLUTEN-FREE

TIME 1 hour, 20 minutes
(20 minutes active)

MAKES 10 to 12 servings

INGREDIENTS

Cooking spray
1 tablespoon canola oil
1 onion, chopped
2 cloves garlic, minced
1 pound lean ground beef
2 teaspoons chili powder
1 teaspoon cumin
1 teaspoon kosher salt
½ teaspoon ground black pepper
2 (14-16-ounce) cans pinto or kidney beans, rinsed and drained
1 (14-16 ounce) can diced fire-roasted tomatoes, drained
1 (4-ounce) can diced green chiles
1 cup frozen corn kernels
½ cup sour cream
1 cup shredded cheddar cheese, divided
1 (32-ounce) bag frozen tater tots

1. Preheat oven to 350 F. Coat a 9x13-inch baking dish with cooking spray.
2. In a large skillet over medium-high heat, warm oil. Saute onion until softened, about 5 minutes, then add garlic and beef; brown beef, breaking up with a spoon, for 8 to 10 minutes. Stir in spices, beans, tomatoes, chiles with their juices, corn, sour cream and ½ cup cheese. Continue to cook for 5 to 7 minutes.
3. Ladle mixture into baking dish. Top with tater tots in a single layer, cover dish with foil, and bake for 30 minutes. Remove foil, sprinkle with remaining cheese, and bake for 20 minutes more.

Streusel-Topped Sweet Potato Casserole

Oats add texture to the traditional brown-sugar topping.

FAMILY FAVORITE | SPECIAL OCCASION

TIME 2 hours, 10 minutes
(10 minutes active)

MAKES 8 to 10 servings

INGREDIENTS

Cooking spray
3 pounds sweet potatoes
¼ cup maple syrup
1½ cups unsalted butter, at room temperature
Zest and juice of half an orange
2½ teaspoons kosher salt, divided
½ teaspoon cinnamon

FOR STREUSEL TOPPING

¼ cup brown sugar
¼ teaspoon cinnamon
¼ cup all-purpose flour
¼ cup old-fashioned oats
¼ cup unsalted butter, diced
¼ cup toasted, chopped pecans

1. Preheat oven to 350 F. Coat a 2-quart baking dish with cooking spray.
2. Roast potatoes until tender (about 1 to 1½ hours). Remove from oven; let cool, then peel and cut into chunks. (Leave oven on.)
3. Meanwhile, make streusel: In a small bowl, mix all ingredients together with your hands. Set aside.
4. In the bowl of a stand mixer fitted with a paddle attachment, whip cool sweet potatoes, syrup, butter, orange zest and juice, salt and cinnamon. Spread mixture in baking dish.
5. Evenly sprinkle streusel over mixture. Bake for 30 minutes or until topping is golden brown.

Cheesy Cauliflower-Broccoli Casserole

A combo of cruciferous veggies adds color to this classic dish.

EASY | FAMILY FAVORITE

TIME 40 minutes
(20 minutes active)

MAKES 8 to 10 servings

INGREDIENTS

Cooking spray
1 head cauliflower, chopped
½ head broccoli, chopped
1 cup whole milk
1 egg, beaten
10 ounces cream cheese, softened
1 cup grated Parmesan cheese
1 cup shredded cheddar cheese
1 teaspoon kosher salt
½ cup panko breadcrumbs
2 tablespoons butter, melted
Fresh parsley, for garnish

1. Preheat oven to 350 F. Coat a 9x13-inch baking dish with cooking spray.
2. Using a steamer basket in a saucepan, steam cauliflower and broccoli until crisp-tender, about 5 minutes. Set aside.
3. In a mixing bowl, whisk together milk, egg and cream cheese. Fold in cheeses. Stir in steamed vegetables and salt. Transfer mixture to baking dish.
4. In a small bowl, stir together breadcrumbs and butter; sprinkle evenly over prepared dish. Bake for 20 minutes or until browned and bubbly. Garnish with parsley.

King Ranch
Chicken
Casserole

King Ranch Chicken Casserole

Toasting the tortillas helps them hold up to the cheesy filling in this spin on a Texas favorite.

EASY | FAMILY FAVORITE | GLUTEN-FREE
TIME 1 hour (10 minutes active)
MAKES 8 to 10 servings

INGREDIENTS

Cooking spray
1 tablespoon canola oil
2 poblano peppers, seeded and chopped
1 red bell pepper, seeded and chopped
1 large red onion, chopped
3 cloves garlic, minced
1 (10.5-ounce) can cream of chicken soup
1 (10.5-ounce) can cream of mushroom soup
1 teaspoon cumin
1 teaspoon chili powder
½ teaspoon kosher salt
¼ teaspoon ground black pepper
3 cups cooked shredded chicken
1 (10-ounce) can diced tomato and green chiles (such as Ro*Tel), drained
¼ cup cilantro, chopped, plus more for garnish
12-14 corn tortillas, lightly toasted and torn in half
1½ cups shredded pepper Jack cheese, divided
1½ cups shredded cheddar cheese, divided

1. Preheat oven to 350 F. Coat a 9x13-inch baking dish with cooking spray.
2. In a large skillet over medium-high heat, warm oil. Add peppers, onion and garlic, and saute until softened, about 5 to 7 minutes. Set aside.
3. In a large mixing bowl, whisk together soups, cumin, chili powder, salt and pepper. Add sauteed vegetables, chicken, tomatoes and cilantro, and fold to combine.
4. Place half of the tortillas in casserole dish. Spread half of the chicken mixture on top. Top with half of the cheese. Repeat layers. Bake for 30 to 40 minutes or until mixture is bubbly and brown. Garnish with cilantro.

French Onion Casserole

Caramelize the onions a day or two ahead and refrigerate.

MAKE-AHEAD | SPECIAL OCCASION
TIME 1 hour, 20 minutes (40 minutes active)
MAKES 8 servings

INGREDIENTS

¼ cup unsalted butter
5 medium onions, thinly sliced
1 teaspoon kosher salt
½ teaspoon ground black pepper
3 thyme sprigs
2 bay leaves
⅓ cup all-purpose flour
3 cups reduced-sodium beef broth
1 teaspoon beef stock base
½ cup sherry
1 baguette, thinly sliced and toasted
8 ounces Gruyere cheese, grated (about 2 cups)
Fresh parsley, chopped, for garnish

1. In a large straight-sided skillet over medium-low heat, melt butter; add onions, salt, pepper, thyme and bay leaves; cook, stirring often, until onions are golden brown, 30 to 40 minutes. Discard thyme and bay leaves.
2. Add flour to onion mixture in skillet and cook, stirring constantly, for 2 minutes. Add broth, stock base and sherry; raise heat to high and bring to a boil. Boil, stirring constantly, until slightly thickened, about 8 to 10 minutes. Meanwhile, preheat oven to 350 F.
3. In a 2-quart baking dish, layer half of the baguette slices. Pour in onion mixture. Top with remaining slices. Sprinkle with cheese; cover with foil.
4. Bake for 30 minutes. Remove foil and broil until cheese is bubbly, about 2 to 3 minutes. Garnish with parsley.

quick tip

To mimic this fish-scale effect, use a round or oval baking dish and place bread slices on topping at an angle, alternating placement with each row.

French
Onion
Casserole

quick tip

To balance balsamic vinegar's tang, use naturally sweet onions, such as Vidalia, for this dish.

Balsamic-Glazed Baked Onions, page 89

chapter eight

Salads & Sides

If you've already got your main
dishes down, look here for inspiration
on what to serve with them.

Cheesy
Baked
Polenta

Cheesy Baked Polenta

Buttery and rich, this side complements any roasted meat-and-vegetable main.

GLUTEN-FREE | SPECIAL OCCASION
TIME 1 hour (30 minutes active)
MAKES 6 to 8 servings

INGREDIENTS

Shortening, for greasing baking dish
2 cups whole milk
2 cups lower-sodium chicken stock
1 cup polenta
1 teaspoon kosher salt
½ teaspoon ground black pepper
1 (8-ounce) block cheddar cheese, grated
1 egg, beaten
¼ cup butter, cut into small pieces
½ cup grated Parmesan cheese

1. Preheat oven to 400 F. Grease a 2-quart baking dish.
2. In a large saucepan over medium-high heat, add milk and stock; bring to a boil. Slowly whisk in polenta and reduce heat to low. Cook, stirring often, until polenta thickens, about 30 minutes. Remove from heat, add salt, pepper, cheddar and egg, whisking to thoroughly combine.
3. Pour polenta mixture into baking dish. Dot top with pats of butter and sprinkle with Parmesan. Bake for 20 to 30 minutes.

quick tip
If you can't find polenta, substitute coarse-ground cornmeal or grits.

Creamed Leeks

Leeks' gentle oniony flavor cuts through the rich cream and cheese sauce.

EASY | GLUTEN-FREE | QUICK
TIME 20 minutes (all active)
MAKES 4 to 6 servings

INGREDIENTS

3 tablespoons unsalted butter
4-6 large leeks, with greens removed, cleaned, halved and sliced
½ teaspoon kosher salt
¼ teaspoon ground black pepper
Pinch of nutmeg
1 cup half-and-half
½ cup grated Parmesan cheese

1. In a large skillet over medium heat, melt butter. Add leeks and saute until softened and most of the water is evaporated, about 10 to 12 minutes.
2. Stir in salt, pepper, nutmeg and half-and-half and simmer, stirring occasionally, until thickened, about 8 to 10 minutes. Stir in cheese just before serving.

Balsamic-Glazed Baked Onions

As the onions roast, they'll soak up the sweet-tart balsamic glaze.

SPECIAL OCCASION | VEGETARIAN
TIME 1 hour (10 minutes active)
MAKES 8 servings

INGREDIENTS

4 small onions
3 tablespoons unsalted butter, melted
½ cup balsamic vinegar
2 tablespoons water
1 tablespoon sugar
½ teaspoon kosher salt
6-8 sprigs fresh thyme, for garnish

1. Preheat oven to 400 F.
2. Slice each onion in half vertically, leaving the root end attached. Carefully peel off the outer papery layers.
3. Into an 8-inch square baking dish, pour butter, vinegar, water, sugar and salt, whisking to combine. Place onions in dish, cut-side up. Wrap dish with foil and bake for 20 minutes. Remove foil, turn onions cut-side down, and bake for 20 to 30 minutes more or until tender.
4. To serve, drizzle with reduced vinegar mixture, if desired and garnish with fresh thyme.

Maple-Roasted Acorn Squash

Acorn squash makes a nice substitute for baked potatoes, if you're looking to mix up your side routine.

EASY | GLUTEN-FREE | VEGETARIAN
TIME 1 hour (50 minutes active)
MAKES 6 servings

INGREDIENTS

3 acorn squash, unpeeled, halved lengthwise and seeded
1½ tablespoons olive oil
2 teaspoons kosher salt
1 teaspoon ground black pepper
3 tablespoons unsalted butter, diced, divided
⅓ cup maple syrup, divided, plus more for drizzling

1. Preheat oven to 350 F.
2. Place squash halves, cut side up, on a rimmed baking sheet. Brush with olive oil and sprinkle with salt and pepper. Place ½ tablespoon butter and 1 tablespoon syrup inside the cavity of each squash. Roast for 45 to 50 minutes or until tender when pierced with a fork.
3. Drizzle with maple syrup to serve.

Ultimate Garlic Mashed Potatoes

Cooking whole cloves of garlic along with the potatoes infuses them with flavor.

FAMILY FAVORITE | GLUTEN-FREE
TIME 40 minutes
(30 minutes active)
MAKES 10 to 12 servings

INGREDIENTS

- 5 pounds Yukon Gold potatoes
- 1 tablespoon plus 2 teaspoons kosher salt, divided
- 5 peeled garlic cloves
- 1 bay leaf
- 1½ cups half-and-half
- ¼ cup butter
- Fresh chives, for garnish

1. Peel potatoes and cut into evenly sized chunks—roughly 2 to 3 inches. Place in a large Dutch oven or stockpot and cover with cold water; add 1 tablespoon salt, garlic and bay leaf. Bring to a boil over high heat; boil vigorously for about 15 minutes or until potatoes are tender when pierced with a fork.
2. Drain, discard bay leaf and place potatoes and garlic back into the still-warm pot. Warm half-and-half in the microwave for 1 minute and add to potatoes, along with butter and remaining 2 teaspoons salt. Whip or mash until smooth, about 5 minutes. Garnish with chives.

4 Ways to Transform Leftover Mashed Potatoes

Sure, you could just eat them again. Or you could try one of these tips.

❶ **POTATO CAKES** Reheat 4 cups mashed potatoes in the microwave, then stir in 2 beaten egg yolks, ½ cup all-purpose flour and ½ cup shredded cheese of your choice. In a nonstick skillet or on a griddle, melt 1 tablespoon butter; drop potato mixture, ¼ cup at a time, into skillet, flatten with a spatula and cook 5 minutes per side.

❷ **DUCHESS POTATOES** Reheat 4 cups mashed potatoes in the microwave, then stir in 2 beaten egg yolks. Place potatoes into a pastry bag equipped with a large star tip. Pipe potatoes in 3-inch-diameter circles on a parchment-lined sheet pan. Bake at 350 F for 20 to 30 minutes or until golden brown.

❸ **SHEPHERD'S PIE TOPPING** Reheat mashed potatoes in the microwave to make spreadable, adding a little liquid if needed, and use as a topping for hearty shepherd's pie. (see page 81.)

❹ **POTATO SOUP** Place mashed potatoes in a saucepan over medium heat and stir in chicken or vegetable stock or milk until you reach the desired consistency. Simmer until warm and top with chives, shredded cheese or crumbled bacon.

Ultimate Garlic Mashed Potatoes

Wilted Spinach With Bacon & Brown Sugar

Salty bacon makes a nice counterpoint to the sweetness of brown sugar and raisins.

EASY | GLUTEN-FREE | QUICK
TIME 15 minutes (all active)
MAKES 4 servings

INGREDIENTS

- 3 slices bacon, chopped
- 2 pounds baby spinach leaves
- 2 tablespoons brown sugar
- ½ teaspoon kosher salt
- ¼ teaspoon ground black pepper
- ¼ cup golden raisins
- Splash apple cider vinegar

1. In a large skillet over medium-high heat, brown bacon, about 5 minutes. Remove bacon with a slotted spoon and set aside to drain.
2. Reduce heat to medium. Add spinach to skillet, sprinkle with sugar, salt and pepper, and turn frequently to wilt the leaves and melt the sugar, about 3 minutes, working in batches if needed.
3. Return bacon to skillet, add raisins and a splash of vinegar, and toss to combine.

Roasted Blue Cheese & Walnut–Stuffed Pears

quick tip
After slicing a pear in half, use a melon baller or a round teaspoon to scoop out the core.

Roasted Blue Cheese & Walnut–Stuffed Pears

Sweet and savory, you can serve this as a starter, side or even a sophisticated dessert.

SPECIAL OCCASION | VEGETARIAN

TIME 40 minutes
(10 minutes active)

MAKES 6 servings

INGREDIENTS

- 3 Bosc pears, unpeeled, halved lengthwise and cored
  Freshly squeezed lemon juice
- 3 ounces crumbled blue cheese
- ¼ cup walnuts, toasted and chopped
- 1 tablespoon fresh rosemary, minced, plus more for garnish
- 1 tablespoon brown sugar
- ½ teaspoon ground black pepper
- 2 tablespoons olive oil
  Honey, for drizzling

1. Preheat oven to 375 F. In a medium bowl, toss pear halves with lemon juice (to prevent browning).
2. In a small bowl, mix cheese, nuts, rosemary, sugar and pepper. Divide mixture evenly between pears, tucking it into the hollow spot where the core was removed. Place pears, cut side up, in a baking dish and drizzle with olive oil.
3. Roast for 20 to 30 minutes or until pears are tender. Garnish with fresh rosemary and some drizzled honey.

Lentil, Carrot & Kale Salad

Top with a fried egg, and this side could easily become a vegetarian main.

Lentil, Carrot & Kale Salad

EASY | GLUTEN-FREE

TIME 40 minutes
(15 minutes active)

MAKES 4 to 6 servings

INGREDIENTS

- ½ pound green lentils, picked, rinsed and drained
- 4 cups curly kale, stemmed and chopped
- 2 tablespoons olive oil
  Juice of half a lemon
- ¼ teaspoon kosher salt
- 2 carrots
- 1 cup pitted Castelvetrano olives, halved
- ½ cup toasted almonds, chopped
- 2 ounces goat cheese, crumbled

1. In a medium saucepan over medium-high heat, add lentils and 4 cups water; when water simmers, turn heat to medium-low and simmer 20 to 30 minutes. Drain and set aside to cool.
2. Meanwhile in a large mixing bowl, add kale; drizzle with oil and lemon juice and sprinkle with salt. With your hands, "massage" the kale to distribute the dressing and soften the kale.
3. Using a peeler, peel carrots, then continue peeling to make long thin strips.
4. In a large serving bowl, toss lentils, carrot strips, olives, almonds and kale; top with goat cheese.

Pomegranate-Roasted Beet Salad

Inspired by an Iranian dish, this salad dresses up any fall table. Roast the red and golden beets in separate packets so their colors don't bleed together.

GLUTEN-FREE | VEGETARIAN
TIME 1 hour, 15 minutes
(15 minutes active)
MAKES 6 to 8 servings

INGREDIENTS

- 4 medium red beets, scrubbed clean with greens removed
- 4 medium golden beets, scrubbed clean with greens removed
- ½ cup pomegranate juice, divided
- 2 tablespoons olive oil, divided, plus more for drizzling
- 2 teaspoons kosher salt, divided
- 8 garlic cloves, divided
- 6 sprigs fresh thyme, divided
- 1½ cups Greek yogurt
  Olive oil, for drizzling
  Fresh dill, for garnish
  Pomegranate arils, for garnish
  Sea salt, for garnish

1. Preheat oven to 400 F.
2. Create two packets with foil that will hold the red and golden beets separately. Into each packet, add the beets, half the pomegranate juice, olive oil, salt, garlic and thyme to each. Tightly fold over foil to seal packets and bake for 40 to 50 minutes, or until beets are tender when pierced with a fork.
3. Open packets and let beets cool for 20 minutes, then peel. (Beets will be easier to peel when slightly warm. Hold over the sink and rub the skins off with paper towels.) Let cool completely and slice into ⅛-inch rounds.
4. Spoon yogurt into a serving dish. Top with sliced beets and garnishes.

Curried Roasted Butternut Squash

Cross-hatching helps the spiced butter seep down into the squash as it roasts, infusing every bite with flavor.

EASY | GLUTEN-FREE | VEGETARIAN
TIME 40 minutes
(10 minutes active)
MAKES 8 servings

INGREDIENTS

- 4 small butternut squash, halved lengthwise and seeded (do not peel)
- ¼ cup unsalted butter, melted
- ¼ cup honey
- 1½ teaspoons kosher salt
- ½ teaspoon ground black pepper
- 1½ teaspoons curry powder
  Chives, for garnish

1. Preheat oven to 400 F.
2. With a paring knife, cut the flesh of each squash half in a cross-hatch pattern. Place squash, cut side up, on a rimmed baking sheet.
3. Place butter and honey in a microwave-safe bowl and microwave in bursts to melt; whisk in salt, pepper and curry. Brush surface of each squash with butter mixture.
4. Roast for 20 to 30 minutes or until tender when pierced with a fork. Garnish with chives.

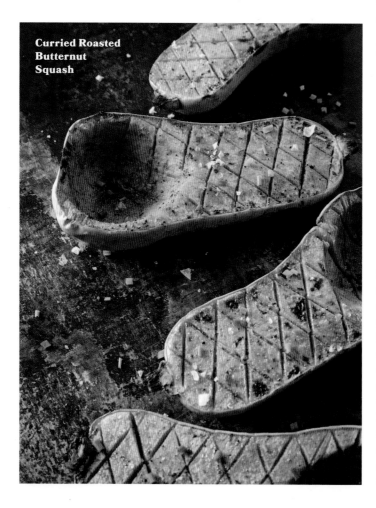

Curried Roasted Butternut Squash

**Pomegranate-
Roasted
Beet Salad**

quick tip

For less mess but all the
flavor, buy pomegranate
juice and arils separately
(both are in the produce
section of most grocers).

quick tip

For even richer flavor, toast farro in a dry skillet over medium heat for a few minutes before cooking.

Farro & Butternut Squash Salad With Smoked Almonds

Farro is an ancient grain with a nutty flavor; the smoked almonds are an ideal complement.

EASY | SPECIAL OCCASION
TIME 40 minutes
(10 minutes active)
MAKES 4 servings

INGREDIENTS

- 2 cups pearled farro
- 1 tablespoon unsalted butter
- 2 cups cubed, peeled butternut squash
- 3 tablespoons olive oil
- 1 tablespoon red wine vinegar
- 1 tablespoon cream cheese, at room temperature
- ½ teaspoon kosher salt
- ¼ teaspoon ground black pepper
- ½ vertically sliced red onion
- ½ cup chopped parsley
- ½ cup chopped smoked almonds

1. Cook farro according to package directions; rinse and set aside to cool.
2. In a large skillet over medium heat, melt butter; add squash and saute until softened, about 12 to 15 minutes.
3. In a small bowl, whisk together oil, vinegar, cream cheese, salt and pepper. In a large serving bowl, toss farro, squash, onion and parsley; toss with oil mixture then top with almonds.

Russet & Sweet Potato Gratin

Blend starchy and sweet potatoes for a beautiful side dish that might steal center stage.

EASY | FAMILY FAVORITE | GLUTEN-FREE
TIME 1 hour, 20 minutes
(15 minutes active)
MAKES 4 servings

INGREDIENTS

Cooking spray
- 2 large sweet potatoes, peeled and sliced into ⅛-inch-thick rounds
- 2 large russet potatoes peeled and sliced into ⅛-inch-thick rounds
- 1½ teaspoons kosher salt
- 1½ cups heavy cream
- ¼ teaspoon nutmeg
- 1½ cups shredded Gruyere cheese, divided
Fresh thyme, for garnish

1. Preheat oven to 400 F. Coat a 2-quart baking dish with cooking spray.
2. In a large mixing bowl, toss potato slices with salt. In a microwave-safe bowl or measuring cup, whisk together cream and nutmeg and microwave for 30 seconds. Pour half of cream mixture into bowl with potatoes and toss to coat.
3. Arrange half of potato mixture in layers (like shingles) inside baking dish; top with half of cheese. Top with remaining potatoes; pour in remaining cream, plus any cream accumulated in the bottom of the potato bowl. Sprinkle with remaining cheese. Cover loosely with foil.
4. Bake for 40 minutes, then remove foil and bake an additional 20 to 25 minutes or until potatoes are tender and cheese is golden brown.

Black-Eyed Peas

Look for black-eyed peas, a Southern staple, in the aisle with other dried beans.

CLASSIC | EASY | GLUTEN-FREE
TIME 1 hour (20 minutes active)
MAKES 8 to 10 servings

INGREDIENTS

- 6 slices bacon, chopped
- 1 green bell pepper, chopped
- 1 onion, chopped
- 3 carrots, peeled and chopped
- 2 celery ribs, chopped
- 3 garlic cloves, minced
- 1 pound dried black-eyed peas, soaked overnight
- 1 bay leaf
- 1 teaspoon smoked paprika
- 3 teaspoons kosher salt, plus more to taste
- 1 jalapeño, halved lengthwise
- 3 cups lower-sodium chicken broth
Sliced scallions, for garnish

1. In a large Dutch oven over medium heat, brown bacon, about 5 minutes. Remove bacon with a slotted spoon and set aside to drain; leave drippings in pan.
2. Saute pepper, onion, carrots, celery and garlic in bacon drippings until softened, about 8 minutes. Stir in peas, bay leaf, paprika, salt and jalapeño. Add chicken broth and enough water to cover peas by 1 inch. Bring to boil, then reduce heat to low; simmer for 40 minutes or until beans are tender.
3. Remove bay leaf and jalapeño before serving.

**Russet & Sweet
Potato Gratin**

**Honey-Ginger
Glazed Carrots &
Parsnips**

quick tip

Look for carrots and
parsnips of similar size,
so they roast evenly.

Honey-Ginger Glazed Carrots & Parsnips

Fresh grated ginger complements root vegetables' natural sweetness.

EASY | GLUTEN-FREE | VEGETARIAN
TIME 30 minutes
(5 minutes active)
MAKES 8 servings

INGREDIENTS

- 2 pounds carrots, peeled, halved lengthwise
- 2 pounds parsnips, peeled, halved lengthwise
- ¼ cup olive oil
- 1 teaspoon kosher salt
- ½ teaspoon ground black pepper
- 1½ tablespoons butter, melted
- 1½ tablespoons honey
- 1 tablespoon fresh grated ginger
  Fresh parsley, for garnish

1. Preheat oven to 425 F.
2. In a large mixing bowl, toss carrots and parsnips with oil. Sprinkle with salt and pepper. Spread carrots and parsnips evenly in a single layer on a rimmed baking sheet.
3. Roast for 20 to 25 minutes, tossing once or twice, until vegetables are tender and slightly browned.
4. In a small bowl, whisk together butter, honey and ginger. Drizzle over roasted vegetables. Garnish with parsley.

Slow-Simmered Fall Greens

This soulful side dish can simmer away happily unattended while you do other tasks.

EASY | GLUTEN-FREE
TIME 2 hours, 10 minutes
(10 minutes active)
MAKES 6 to 8 servings

INGREDIENTS

- 2 pounds collard, turnip or mustard greens (or a mix), chopped with stems removed
- 1 jalapeño pepper, halved
- 1 smoked ham hock
- 1 tablespoon kosher salt
- 1 teaspoon ground black pepper

1. In a large Dutch oven or stockpot, add greens and cover with water by 1 inch. Add jalapeño, hock, salt and pepper. Cook on high until boiling, then reduce to low to simmer. Cook 2 hours.
2. To serve, remove hock and jalapeño.

Brussels Sprout & Apple Slaw

Julienned apples balance the tart, vinegary dressing.

GLUTEN-FREE | QUICK | VEGETARIAN
TIME 15 minutes (all active)
MAKES 6 servings

INGREDIENTS

- 1 pound Brussels sprouts, shredded
- 2 carrots, peeled and shredded
- 3 scallions, thinly sliced
- 2 Honeycrisp or Pink Lady apples, cut into matchsticks
  Freshly squeezed lemon juice
- 2 tablespoons whole-grain mustard
- 2 tablespoons mayonnaise
- ¼ cup apple cider vinegar
- 1 tablespoon sugar
- 1 teaspoon kosher salt
- ½ teaspoon ground black pepper
- ½ teaspoon celery seeds

1. In a large serving bowl, toss sprouts, carrots and scallions to combine. In a separate bowl, toss apples with lemon juice to prevent browning; add to sprouts mixture.
2. In a small bowl, whisk together remaining ingredients to make dressing; fold into slaw.

Brussels Sprout & Apple Slaw

9-Layer Fall Salad

Put an autumn spin on the summertime picnic staple. Prepare the ingredients ahead of time and assemble when ready.

EASY | GLUTEN-FREE | MAKE-AHEAD
TIME 30 minutes
(10 minutes active)
MAKES 10 to 12 servings

INGREDIENTS

- ½ cup quinoa, rinsed
- 2 heads iceberg lettuce, chopped
- ½ pound kale, stemmed and chopped
- 2 (12-ounce) jars roasted red peppers, drained and chopped
- 8 hard-boiled eggs, chopped
- 12 ounces bacon, cooked and chopped
- 1 bunch scallions, thinly sliced
- 1 (8-ounce) block white cheddar cheese, grated
- 1 cup chopped toasted pecans

FOR DRESSING

- ½ cup mayonnaise
- ½ cup sour cream
- 1 tablespoon sugar
- ¼ cup chopped parsley

1. In a medium saucepan over medium-high heat, add quinoa and 1 cup water; when water simmers, turn heat to medium-low and simmer until tender, about 15 minutes. Drain and set aside to cool.

quick tip

Add roasted chicken or shrimp to make this citrusy spinach salad a main dish.

2. Meanwhile, place dressing ingredients in a Mason jar and shake well to combine.
3. In a large (3-quart or more) straight-sided glass bowl, layer ingredients in order, starting with quinoa. Top with dressing. To serve, stir dressing into salad.

Orange-Avocado Salad With Cider Vinaigrette

EASY | GLUTEN-FREE | QUICK
TIME 10 minutes (all active)
MAKES 2 servings

INGREDIENTS

- 1 orange, peeled and sliced
- 1 ruby grapefruit, peeled and sliced into segments
- 1 avocado, peeled, seed removed and sliced into segments
- 2 cups baby spinach leaves
- 1 small shallot, sliced into rings
- ¼ cup toasted hazelnuts, roughly chopped
- ¼ cup pepitas (pumpkin seeds)
- 4 dates, sliced into rings
  Kosher salt and ground black pepper, to taste

FOR VINAIGRETTE

- ¾ cup extra-virgin olive oil
- ¼ cup apple cider vinegar
- 1 tablespoon Dijon mustard
- 1 teaspoon honey
- 1 small shallot, minced
- 1 teaspoon kosher salt
- ½ teaspoon ground black pepper

1. On a serving plate, arrange sliced fruits, avocado and spinach. Top with shallot, nuts, pepitas and dates. Season with salt and pepper.
2. To make vinaigrette, place all ingredients in a Mason jar and shake well to combine.

Orange-Avocado Salad With Cider Vinaigrette

5 Vinaigrette Variations
Whip up a fresh dressing.

① RED WINE & PARMESAN Whisk together ¾ cup extra-virgin olive oil, ¼ cup red wine vinegar, 1 tablespoon whole grain mustard, 2 tablespoons finely grated Parmesan cheese, 1 teaspoon honey, 1 minced garlic clove, 1 teaspoon kosher salt and ½ teaspoon black pepper.

② BALSAMIC & ORANGE Whisk together ¾ cup extra-virgin olive oil, ¼ cup balsamic vinegar, 1 tablespoon Dijon mustard, zest and juice of half an orange, 1 small shallot, minced, 1 teaspoon kosher salt and ½ teaspoon black pepper.

③ SWEET ONION Whisk together ¾ cup canola oil, ¼ cup white vinegar, 2 tablespoons finely grated sweet onion, 2 tablespoons sugar, 1 teaspoon kosher salt, ½ teaspoon black pepper and ¼ teaspoon celery seed.

④ CREAMY LEMON & DILL Whisk together ¾ cup extra-virgin olive oil, ¼ cup fresh lemon juice, 1 tablespoon mayonnaise, 1 teaspoon honey, 1 small minced shallot, 1 tablespoon minced fresh dill, 1 tablespoon fresh minced parsley, 1 teaspoon kosher salt and ½ teaspoon black pepper.

⑤ SESAME-GINGER Whisk together ½ cup canola oil, ¼ cup toasted sesame oil, ¼ cup rice wine vinegar, 1 tablespoon grated fresh ginger, 1 minced garlic clove and 1 teaspoon kosher salt.

quick tip

Pouring the batter into a preheated skillet gives this rustic bread its signature crust.

Southern-Style
Skillet Cornbread,
page 104

chapter nine

Breads

Flex your creativity—and your kneading muscles—with a variety of quick, under-an-hour loaves or all-afternoon baking projects.

Cinnamon Swirl Loaf

The pretty results are worth the wait!

FAMILY FAVORITE | SPECIAL OCCASION

TIME 3 hours, 15 minutes (30 minutes active)

MAKES 1 loaf

INGREDIENTS

- 3 cups all-purpose flour, plus more for dusting
- ¼ cup nonfat powdered milk
- 1¼ teaspoons kosher salt
- ½ teaspoon cinnamon
- 3 tablespoons sugar
- 2½ teaspoons instant yeast
- 4 tablespoons butter
- 1 cup lukewarm water
  Cooking spray or shortening, for greasing bowl, pan and work surface

FOR THE FILLING

- ½ cup sugar
- 3 teaspoons cinnamon
- 4 teaspoons all-purpose flour
- 1 egg, beaten

1. In a mixing bowl, combine all dough ingredients. Mix and knead everything together by hand, or with a stand mixer with a dough hook attachment, until a smooth dough forms, about 5 to 8 minutes.
2. Lightly coat a bowl with cooking spray. Place dough in bowl, cover, and let rise at room temperature until doubled in bulk, about 1 hour.
3. While dough rises, make filling: In a small bowl, whisk together sugar, cinnamon and flour.
4. Lightly coat work surface and an 8½- x 4½-inch loaf pan with cooking spray. Transfer risen dough to work surface and roll into an 8x20-inch rectangle. Stir a teaspoon or two of water into beaten egg; brush dough with egg mixture and evenly sprinkle filling on top, leaving a 1-inch border on both sides and one 8-inch end.
5. Beginning with the filled 8-inch edge, roll dough into a log. Pinch the seam and ends closed, and place the log into prepared loaf pan. Cover loosely with plastic wrap and let rise until dough reaches the top of the pan, about 1 hour. Preheat oven to 350 F.
6. Bake for 40 to 45 minutes, loosely tenting with foil, if needed, to prevent over-browning. Remove from oven, let bread sit for 5 minutes, then gently turn out of pan and let cool on a rack.

Ginger-Cinnamon-Maple Monkey Bread Muffins

A less-mess version of the popular gooey treat—and everybody gets their own serving.

EASY | SPECIAL OCCASION

TIME 25 minutes (10 minutes active)

MAKES 12 muffins

INGREDIENTS

- Cooking spray
- 2 tablespoons sugar
- 2 teaspoons cinnamon
- ½ teaspoon powdered ginger
  Pinch ground cloves
- 1 (12-ounce) can biscuit dough (such as Pillsbury)
- ¼ cup butter
- 2 tablespoons light brown sugar, packed
- 2 tablespoons maple syrup

1. Preheat oven to 350 F. Lightly coat a 12-count muffin tin with cooking spray.
2. In a large mixing bowl, stir together sugar, cinnamon, ginger and cloves. Separate each biscuit into 6 pieces; toss in sugar mixture to coat. Place 5 pieces of sugared dough into each muffin cup.
3. In a microwave-safe liquid measuring cup, melt butter, sugar and syrup in short bursts, stirring to combine. Pour 1½ teaspoons into each prepared muffin cup. Bake 15 minutes or until golden brown. Cool 2 to 3 minutes in the pan, then remove.

---

quick tip

For Monkey Bread Muffins, be sure to pack brown sugar firmly into the measuring cup to get the correct amount. Spoon it into the cup, then use the back of the spoon to press.

Southern-Style Skillet Cornbread

This is perfect with chili on a cool night.

EASY | FAMILY FAVORITE

TIME 30 minutes (5 minutes active)

MAKES 1 (10-inch) round

INGREDIENTS

- 2 tablespoons shortening
- 2 cups coarse-ground cornmeal
- 1 teaspoon kosher salt
- 1 teaspoon baking powder
- 1 teaspoon baking soda
- 1½ cups buttermilk
- 2 eggs, beaten
- 2 tablespoons butter, melted

1. Preheat oven to 400 F. Add shortening to a 10-inch skillet and place in oven to heat.

Cinnamon Swirl Loaf

2. In a mixing bowl, whisk together cornmeal, salt, baking powder and baking soda. In a liquid measuring cup, whisk together buttermilk, eggs and butter. Pour liquid ingredients into cornmeal mixture, stirring to combine. (Batter may be lumpy—that's OK.)

3. Carefully remove hot skillet from oven and swirl melted shortening to coat sides. Pour batter into skillet and return to oven. Bake for 20 to 25 minutes. Serve it straight from the pan.

5 Flavor-Boosting Cornbread Additions

Kick up the basic recipe with any of these combinations.

❶ CHEDDAR & JALAPEÑO Stir 1 cup shredded cheddar cheese and 1 small seeded and chopped jalapeño into the batter.

❷ CHIPOTLE Dice 2 canned chipotle peppers in adobo and add to wet ingredients.

❸ SCALLION & BACON Chop 5 scallions and 2 strips of cooked and cooled bacon and toss with the dry ingredients.

❹ ORANGE & CRANBERRY Toss ½ cup dried cranberries with dry ingredients; stir zest of half an orange into wet ingredients.

❺ SAGE Add 1 teaspoon rubbed sage to the dry ingredients; top batter with 5 small sage leaves in a decorative pattern once poured into the skillet.

Sour Cream Beer Bread

The combination of self-rising flour and beer supplies the lift for these loaves.

EASY | FAMILY FAVORITE

TIME 45 minutes
(5 minutes active)

MAKES 2 loaves

INGREDIENTS

Shortening, for greasing loaf pans

5 cups self-rising flour

5 tablespoons sugar

1 (12-ounce) bottle lager- or pilsner-style beer

12 ounces sour cream

2 tablespoons butter, melted

Sea salt, for sprinkling

1. Preheat oven to 350 F. Grease two 8½- x 4½-inch loaf pans with shortening.

2. In a large mixing bowl, whisk together flour and sugar; whisk in beer and sour cream.

3. Pour batter into prepared loaf pans. Bake for 30 minutes. Remove from oven and pour melted butter over top of each loaf and sprinkle with sea salt. Bake 10 minutes more. Let cool on wire rack.

Rosemary & Olive Focaccia

Top this with cherry tomatoes, too.

FAMILY FAVORITE | SPECIAL OCCASION

TIME 2 hours, 20 minutes
(20 minutes active)

MAKES About 12 servings

INGREDIENTS

- 1 cup warm water
- 2¼ teaspoons instant yeast (1 packet)
- 2 tablespoons honey
- 3½ cups all-purpose flour
- ½ teaspoon salt
- ½ teaspoon garlic powder
- ¼ cup olive oil, divided
- 1 cup pitted Kalamata olives, drained and halved
- 1 tablespoon rosemary leaves
  Sea salt, for sprinkling

1. In a liquid measuring cup, combine water, yeast and honey, stirring to dissolve; set aside for 5 to 8 minutes or until foamy.
2. In the bowl of a stand mixer with a dough hook attachment, combine flour, salt and garlic powder, then add 1 tablespoon oil and slowly pour in yeast mixture. Knead until dough comes together, about 8 to 10 minutes. If needed, add additional flour, 1 tablespoon at a time. Pour 1 tablespoon oil into a large mixing bowl, swirling to coat; place dough inside, cover, and let rise about 45 minutes or until doubled in size.
3. Drizzle sheet pan with 1 tablespoon oil. Shape dough into 10x14-inch oval. Cover and let rise again, about 45 minutes. Use fingertips to lightly dimple surface, drizzle with remaining oil, arrange olives and rosemary on top, and sprinkle with salt.
4. Preheat oven to 350 F. Bake for 20 to 25 minutes or until golden brown. Remove from pan and let cool on a rack.

Pumpkin-Molasses Bread

This bread is moist and rich as is, and even better with one of our Sweet Stir-Ins (see sidebar).

EASY | FAMILY FAVORITE

TIME 1 hour, 45 minutes
(15 minutes active)

MAKES 2 loaves

INGREDIENTS

- Cooking spray
- 1 cup canola or vegetable oil
- 2 cups sugar
- ¼ cup unsulphured molasses
- 4 eggs, at room temperature
- 1 (15-ounce) can pumpkin puree
- ⅔ cup skim milk
- ½ teaspoon vanilla extract
- 3½ cups all-purpose flour
- ½ teaspoon baking powder
- 1 teaspoon baking soda
- 1½ teaspoons kosher salt
- 1 teaspoon nutmeg
  Turbinado sugar, for sprinkling

1. Preheat oven to 350 F. Lightly coat two 8½- x 4½-inch loaf pans with cooking spray.
2. Using a large mixing bowl and hand mixer, or a stand mixer with a paddle attachment, beat together oil, sugar, molasses, eggs, pumpkin, milk and vanilla. In a separate bowl, whisk together flour, baking powder, baking soda, salt and nutmeg. Gradually add flour mixture to oil mixture until fully combined.
3. Divide batter between loaf pans. Sprinkle tops with turbinado sugar. Bake for 1 hour or until a tester inserted into the center of each loaf comes out clean. Cool pans on a rack for 30 minutes, then gently turn out onto rack to cool fully.

5 Sweet Stir-Ins For Pumpkin Bread

Amp up the flavor—and the accolades—with any one of these additions.

1 CHOCOLATE CHIP Toss 1 cup semisweet chocolate morsels with 1 tablespoon all-purpose flour. Stir into batter after all the flour mixture is incorporated, then bake as directed.

2 CRANBERRY Toss 1 cup dried cranberries with 1 tablespoon all-purpose flour. Stir into batter after all the flour mixture is incorporated, then bake as directed.

3 NUTELLA Fill pans halfway with batter, then spoon 3 tablespoons of chocolate-hazelnut spread (such as Nutella) into each, swirling with a knife. Top with remaining batter and bake as directed.

4 CRUMBLE-TOPPED In a bowl, combine ½ cup light brown sugar, ½ cup old-fashioned rolled oats, ¼ cup all-purpose flour, ¼ cup room temperature unsalted butter and ½ teaspoon cinnamon with your hands. Sprinkle evenly over prepared loaves and bake as directed.

5 MAPLE-GLAZED In a bowl, whisk together 1 cup sifted powdered sugar and 2 teaspoons maple syrup. Slowly pour in 1 tablespoon water, whisking constantly, until pourable (add more water 1 teaspoon at a time, if needed). Pour over cooled loaves.

Cranberry & Walnut Loaf

As homemade bread goes, this is a beginner-friendly option that everyone will love. It comes together quickly, too; most of the time is in the rising.

EASY | FAMILY FAVORITE
TIME 12 hours (20 minutes active)
MAKES 1 loaf

INGREDIENTS

- 4¼ cups bread flour
- 2 teaspoons kosher salt
- ½ teaspoon instant yeast
- 1¾ cups water
- ½ cup dried cranberries
- ½ cup dried currants
- ½ cup raisins
- ½ cup chopped, toasted walnuts
  Butter or shortening, for greasing pan

1. In a large mixing bowl, combine flour, salt, yeast and water with your hands to form a sticky dough. Add fruits and walnuts, and continue to work dough with your hands to evenly distribute. Cover bowl with plastic wrap and let dough rise overnight at room temperature.

2. Lightly grease a 9- or 10-inch round cast-iron Dutch oven with butter or shortening. Turn dough out onto a lightly floured surface and shape to fit the pan. Place dough inside, cover with lid and let rise again for 2 hours.

3. Cover pan and place on bottom rack of cold oven. Set to 450 F and bake 45 to 50 minutes. Remove lid and bake 10 minutes more, or until golden brown on top. Let Dutch oven cool for 10 minutes, then carefully turn bread out onto a rack to cool completely.

Cranberry & Walnut Loaf

Orange-Ginger Pull-Apart Bread

Each layer is separated by a buttery, gingery filling; turmeric gives the loaf extra color.

FAMILY FAVORITE | SPECIAL OCCASION
TIME 3 hours (45 minutes active)
MAKES 1 loaf

INGREDIENTS

- 6 tablespoons butter
- 1 cup milk
- ¾ cup sugar
- 1 tablespoon instant yeast
- 4 cups all-purpose flour, plus more for dusting
- 1 teaspoon turmeric
- ½ teaspoon salt
- 1 egg, beaten
  Cooking spray, for greasing pan and work surface

FOR THE FILLING

- ⅓ cup butter, softened
- 1 orange, zested and juice from half
- 2 tablespoons grated ginger

FOR THE GLAZE

- 1 tablespoon boiling water
- 1 tablespoon sugar
- 1 tablespoon orange juice

1. In a microwave-safe bowl, add butter, milk and sugar; heat in bursts until melted. Stir together to combine and let sit until lukewarm (about 100 F to 110 F). Sprinkle yeast into bowl and let sit to activate. After a few minutes, bubbles should appear on the surface. (If they don't, repeat with fresh yeast.)

2. In a mixing bowl, whisk together flour, turmeric and salt. Pour in yeast mixture and egg. Mix and knead everything together—by hand or with a stand mixer and dough hook—until a smooth dough forms, about 5 to 8 minutes. Lightly spray a

medium bowl with cooking spray and place dough in bowl. Cover and let rise at room temperature until doubled in bulk, about 1 hour.

3. While dough rises, make filling: In a small bowl, stir together butter, orange zest and juice, and ginger.

4. Lightly coat a work surface and an 8½- x 4½-inch loaf pan with cooking spray. Transfer risen dough to work surface and roll into a 16x20-inch rectangle. Spread filling evenly over dough's surface. Cut dough crosswise into 8 strips (each 2 inches wide). Stack two strips on top of each other. Cut each strip into 5 equal-size rectangles that are slightly narrower than the width of the pan (each should be 2 inches by 4 inches). Layer the dough squares upright in pan. Cover and let rest for 30 minutes. Meanwhile, preheat oven to 375 F.

5. Bake for 40 to 45 minutes, loosely tenting with foil, if needed, to prevent over-browning. Meanwhile, in a small bowl, stir together glaze ingredients. Remove loaf from oven, brush with glaze and let sit for 10 minutes, then gently turn out of the pan and place on a rack to cool.

Orange-Ginger Pull-Apart Bread

Overnight Sourdough Crescent Rolls

There's nothing wrong with the ones that come in a can. But if you want to try your hand at making homemade crescent rolls, start here.

FAMILY FAVORITE | SPECIAL OCCASION
TIME 12 hours (30 minutes active)
MAKES 36 rolls

INGREDIENTS

- 1 cup warm water
- ½ cup sugar
- 2¼ teaspoons instant yeast (1 packet)
- 2 eggs, beaten
- 1 teaspoon kosher salt
- ½ cup butter, at room temperature
- 4 cups sifted all-purpose flour, more for dusting
  Cooking spray

1. In a large mixing bowl, combine water, sugar and yeast, stirring to dissolve; set aside for 30 minutes. Stir in eggs, salt, butter and flour. Cover with a kitchen towel and let stand overnight at room temperature.

2. Divide risen dough into 3 equal parts. On a lightly floured surface, roll each portion into a 10-inch circle. With a sharp knife or pizza wheel, cut each circle into 12 wedges. Starting at the large end, roll up each wedge and shape each roll into a crescent.

3. Lightly coat rimless baking sheets with cooking spray. Place rolls on baking sheets; cover and let rise for 2 hours or until they appear puffy.

4. Preheat oven to 350 F. Bake for 10 minutes or until golden brown. Serve warm.

Sweet Potato Layer Cake With Cream Cheese Frosting, page 112

☀

quick tip

Spoon a dollop of frosting into the center of your cake stand before stacking and decorating; it will help hold the cake in place.

chapter ten

Desserts

Every gathering deserves a happy
ending, whether it's a towering layer cake,
gooey homemade caramel sauce
over ice cream or a stack of dressed-up
brownies made from a boxed mix.

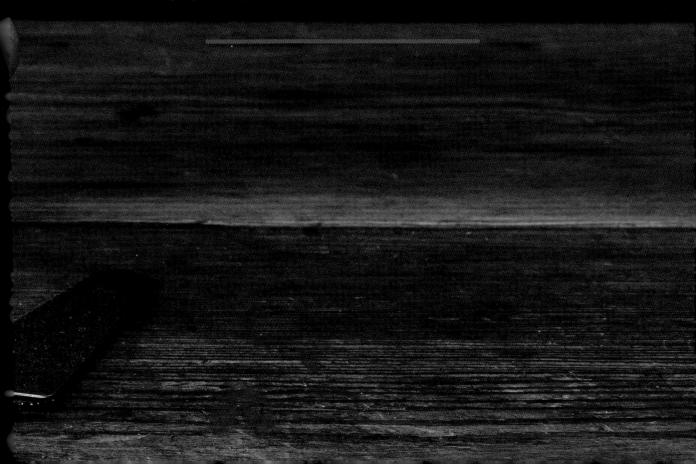

DESSERTS

Sweet Potato Layer Cake With Cream Cheese Frosting

Using oil instead of butter makes for an especially moist cake.

FAMILY FAVORITE | SPECIAL OCCASION
TIME 2 hours, 15 minutes
(1 hour active)
MAKES 1 cake

INGREDIENTS

Butter or shortening, for greasing pans
4 eggs, separated
1½ cups sugar
1 cup vegetable or canola oil
2¾ cups cake flour, sifted, plus more for dusting
1 tablespoon baking powder
½ teaspoon kosher salt
2 teaspoons cinnamon
1 teaspoon powdered ginger
½ teaspoon ground cloves
1½ cups finely grated peeled sweet potato
½ cup chopped walnuts
¼ cup hot water

FOR THE FROSTING

8 ounces cream cheese, at room temperature
¼ cup unsalted butter, at room temperature
2 cups powdered sugar, sifted
1 teaspoon vanilla extract
2 tablespoons whole milk
1 cup finely chopped toasted pecans

1. Preheat oven to 350 F. Grease and flour three 8-inch round cake pans.
2. In the bowl of a stand mixer fitted with a whisk attachment, or with a hand mixer, beat egg whites until stiff peaks form, about 5 minutes; remove from bowl and set aside.
3. Wipe out the bowl with a paper towel, add paddle attachment to stand mixer and beat sugar and oil on medium speed, scraping down the sides as needed, about 8 to 10 minutes. Add egg yolks, one at a time. In a medium mixing bowl, whisk together flour, baking powder, salt and spices. Gradually add flour mixture to sugar mixture, then stir in sweet potato, nuts and water. Fold in beaten egg whites.
4. Divide batter evenly between cake pans. Bake for 30 to 35 minutes or until a tester inserted into the center of each cake comes out clean. Cool cakes in pans for 10 minutes, then carefully turn out onto a rack and cool completely, about 1 hour.
5. To make frosting, in a stand mixer with the paddle attachment, or with a hand mixer, beat cream cheese and butter. Gradually add sugar, beating until smooth with each addition. Add vanilla and continue beating until fluffy. Add milk 1 tablespoon at a time until frosting is thick and spreadable (you may not use all of the milk). Beat for 3 to 5 minutes on high speed until fluffy.
6. Spread between each layer and on top of cake. Sprinkle top with pecans.

Pumpkin Bread Pudding With Honey-Bourbon Whipped Cream

To make an entire pan instead of individual servings, use a 2½-quart baking dish and add about 10 minutes to the baking time (check to make sure the center is set).

MAKE-AHEAD | SPECIAL OCCASION
TIME 1 hour, 10 minutes
(10 minutes active)
MAKES 4 servings

INGREDIENTS

Cooking spray
6 large eggs
2 cups half-and-half
1 cup whole milk
1 (15-ounce) can pumpkin puree
½ cup granulated sugar
¼ cup light brown sugar, packed
¼ cup molasses
¼ cup bourbon
½ teaspoon kosher salt
1 teaspoon cinnamon, plus more for dusting
¼ teaspoon cloves
⅛ teaspoon nutmeg
1 teaspoon vanilla extract
8 cups cubed day-old white bread

1. Coat four (8- to 10-ounce) ramekins or individual-sized baking dishes.
2. In a large mixing bowl, whisk eggs, then whisk in half-and-half, milk, pumpkin, sugars, molasses, bourbon, salt, spices and vanilla. Set aside.
3. Divide bread evenly among ramekins. Pour egg mixture evenly over bread and let rest at room temperature for 20 to 30 minutes so egg mixture is absorbed.
4. Preheat oven to 350 F. Bake 20 to 30 minutes or until golden brown and centers are firm. Serve warm topped with Honey-Bourbon Whipped Cream (recipe follows); dust with cinnamon.

HONEY-BOURBON WHIPPED CREAM

In a medium bowl, with a hand mixer or a stand mixer with a whisk attachment on low speed, mix together 1 cup cold heavy cream, 1 teaspoon honey and 1 teaspoon bourbon. Set speed to high after mixing, then whip until soft peaks form, about 2 minutes.

quick tip

For the best texture and
maximum fluffy volume,
make sure your heavy
cream is thoroughly
chilled before whipping.

**Pumpkin Bread
Pudding With
Honey-Bourbon
Whipped Cream**

Pecan Blondies

If you can't find pecan butter, make your own: In a food processor or high-powered blender, blitz 2 cups of toasted pecans with a pinch of salt for 8 to 10 minutes or until smooth and creamy.

EASY | FAMILY FAVORITE

TIME 1 hour, 10 minutes (10 minutes active)

MAKES 16 to 20 servings

INGREDIENTS

Cooking spray
¾ cup unsalted butter
¾ cup pecan butter
½ teaspoon kosher salt
3 cups light brown sugar
4 eggs, at room temperature
1 teaspoon vanilla extract
3½ cups all-purpose flour
½ cup pecan halves
Sea salt, for sprinkling

1. Preheat oven to 325 F. Coat a 9x13-inch baking dish with cooking spray.
2. In a microwave-safe mixing bowl, add butter and pecan butter. Microwave for 2 minutes to melt; whisk together to blend.
3. Using a stand mixer with a paddle attachment, or a hand mixer, beat in sugar, then eggs, one at a time. Stir in vanilla, then gradually add flour.
4. Pour batter into baking dish. Top with pecan halves and sprinkle with sea salt. Bake for 1 hour, 20 minutes. Let cool completely in the pan, then slice.

Cranberry Pretzel Salad

A little sweet, a little salty...this has something for everybody.

EASY | FAMILY FAVORITE

TIME 12 hours
(20 minutes active)

MAKES 12 servings

INGREDIENTS

- 6 cups pretzels, finely crushed
- ¾ cup butter, melted
- ¼ cup sugar
- 1 (6-ounce) package Black Cherry Jell-O
- 1 (14-ounce) can jellied cranberry sauce
- 1 cup heavy cream, whipped
- 8 ounces cream cheese, at room temperature
- 1 cup powdered sugar

1. Preheat oven to 350 F. Coat a 9x13-inch baking dish with cooking spray.
2. In a mixing bowl, combine pretzels, butter and sugar. Pour mixture into baking dish. Flatten mixture with fingers to form an even crust. Bake for 8 to 10 minutes or until set. Set aside to cool.
3. In a large mixing bowl, prepare Jell-O according to package directions; whisk in cranberry sauce and refrigerate for 4 to 5 hours or until partially set (mixture should be thickened, but still able to be stirred).
4. In a stand mixer with a whisk attachment, whip cream until soft peaks form, about 4 to 6 minutes. Remove whipped cream to a separate bowl; set aside.
5. In the same mixer bowl with a paddle attachment, whip cream cheese and sugar until well blended. Fold whipped cream into cream cheese mixture.
6. Spread cream cheese mixture on top of cooled crust. Spoon thickened Jell-O mixture on top of cream cheese mixture. Cover and refrigerate overnight to set.

**Brown-Sugar
Pound Cake
With Maple Glaze**

Brown-Sugar Pound Cake With Maple Glaze

Brown sugar gives this favorite a richer caramel flavor.

FAMILY FAVORITE | SPECIAL OCCASION

TIME 1 hour, 45 minutes
(15 minutes active)

MAKES 16 servings

INGREDIENTS

- 1½ cups unsalted butter, at room temperature, plus more for greasing the pan
- 8 ounces cream cheese, at room temperature
- 2 cups sugar
- 1½ cups light brown sugar
- 1 teaspoon kosher salt
- 6 eggs, at room temperature
- 2 teaspoons vanilla extract
- 3 cups cake flour, sifted, plus more for flouring the pan

1. Preheat oven to 325 F. Grease and flour a 10-inch tube pan.
2. In the bowl of a stand mixer fitted with a paddle attachment, on medium-high speed, beat butter, cream cheese, sugars and salt until fluffy, scraping down the sides as needed, about 8 to 10 minutes.
3. On medium speed, add eggs one at a time until fully incorporated. Add vanilla. Gradually add flour until combined.
4. Pour batter into prepared pan and bake for 1 hour 15 minutes or until a tester comes out clean. Cool on a rack for 10 to 15 minutes, then carefully turn out and return to rack to fully cool. Glaze cake with Maple Glaze (recipe follows) when cool; pour extra glaze over individual servings.

MAPLE GLAZE

In a mixing bowl, whisk together 1 cup sifted confectioners' sugar and 2 teaspoons maple syrup. Slowly pour in 1 tablespoon water, whisking constantly, until mixture becomes glossy and thick, but pourable (add more water 1 teaspoon at a time, if needed).

Apple Date Cakes

These moist, rich cakes are dense with fruit and topped with a crackly, buttery crust.

EASY | FAMILY FAVORITE

TIME 1 hour, 30 minutes
(20 minutes active)

MAKES 2 loaves

INGREDIENTS

Shortening and flour, for greasing and flouring pans
¾ cup butter, softened
2 cups sugar
2 eggs
2 cups all-purpose flour, plus 1 tablespoon, divided
1 teaspoon baking soda
1 teaspoon baking powder
¼ teaspoon kosher salt
¾ teaspoon cinnamon
1 cup dates, chopped
1 cup pecans, chopped
2 apples, peeled, cored and chopped

1. Preheat oven to 325 F. Grease and flour two 4½- x 8½-inch loaf pans.
2. In the bowl of a stand mixer with paddle attachment, or using a hand mixer, cream butter and sugar until fluffy. Beat in eggs.
3. In a medium bowl, whisk together 2 cups flour, baking soda, baking powder, salt and cinnamon; gradually beat into butter mixture. (The batter will be very stiff.)

quick tip

Pinch together any tears in the dough that may form when folding. Reseal them with extra egg wash.

4. In a small bowl, toss dates with remaining flour to prevent them from clumping; stir dates, pecans and apples into batter. Spread batter in loaf pans.
5. Bake for 1 hour and 10 minutes. Cool on a rack before removing from pans.

No-Bake Sweet Potato Peanut Butter Swirls

The sweet potato provides just enough moisture to bind the soft dough together.

EASY | GLUTEN-FREE

TIME 2 hours, 15 minutes
(15 minutes active)

MAKES About 30 candies

INGREDIENTS

1 small sweet potato, cooked, cooled and peeled
1 teaspoon vanilla
2 teaspoons maple syrup
1½-2 cups confectioners' sugar, sifted, plus more for dusting
½ cup creamy peanut butter

1. In a stand mixer with paddle attachment, or using a hand mixer, beat potato pulp until completely smooth, about 3 minutes. Add vanilla and syrup. Gradually add sugar, 1 cup at a time, until a soft dough forms, adjusting with more if needed.
2. Lightly sprinkle a sheet of waxed paper with powdered sugar. Place dough on top; press to flatten slightly, sprinkle with more sugar, then place more waxed paper on top. Roll the dough between the two sheets into an 8- x 10-inch rectangle about ¼-inch thick.
3. Remove top sheet of wax paper and spread peanut butter on dough surface. Roll dough into a log, using the paper to help shape. Wrap rolled dough in wax paper and refrigerate for at least 2 hours or overnight.

4. Slice into ¼-inch thick pieces. Store in an airtight container between sheets of wax paper for up to 5 days.

Pear Galette

Be careful not to tear the dough when folding so the filling remains inside this free-form pie as it bakes.

EASY | SPECIAL OCCASION

TIME 1 hour
(10 minutes active)

MAKES 8 servings

INGREDIENTS

1 roll refrigerated pie dough
All-purpose flour, for dusting
2 small pears, cored and sliced
Zest and juice of half a lemon
2 teaspoons cornstarch
⅓ cup sugar
2 tablespoons light brown sugar
¾ teaspoon cinnamon
⅛ teaspoon nutmeg
1 egg, beaten
Turbinado sugar, for sprinkling

1. Preheat oven to 375 F. Line a rimmed baking sheet with parchment.
2. On a lightly floured surface, roll dough into a 10-inch circle. Place dough on baking sheet.
3. In a mixing bowl, toss pears with lemon zest and juice, cornstarch, sugars, cinnamon and nutmeg. Starting about 1 to 2 inches from edge of dough, arrange pears in a circular pattern, overlapping edges.
4. Fold edges of dough toward center, forming overlapping pleats. Brush crust with egg and sprinkle with turbinado sugar. Bake for 45 to 50 minutes or until golden and bubbly. Let cool completely before slicing.

Pear Galette

Spiced Molasses Cookies

Warm notes of cinnamon, clove and ginger infuse every bite.

EASY | FAMILY FAVORITE

TIME 30 minutes
(15 minutes active)

MAKES About 16 cookies

INGREDIENTS

- 2¼ cups all-purpose flour
- 1 teaspoon baking soda
- 2 teaspoons cinnamon
- 1 teaspoon ground cloves
- ½ teaspoon nutmeg
- ½ teaspoon ground ginger
- ¼ teaspoon kosher salt
- 1 cup dark brown sugar, packed
- ¼ cup vegetable oil
- ⅓ cup unsulfured molasses
- 1 egg, at room temperature
  Turbinado sugar, for rolling cookies

1. Preheat oven to 350 F. Line 2 baking sheets with parchment.

2. In a mixing bowl, whisk together flour, baking soda, cinnamon, cloves, nutmeg and salt.

3. In the bowl of a stand mixer with a paddle attachment, or using a hand mixer, beat sugar, oil and molasses on medium speed for 5 minutes. Add egg and mix on low for 1 minute, scraping the bowl with a rubber spatula if needed. Gradually add flour mixture to sugar mixture and mix until combined.

4. Place turbinado sugar in a wide, shallow dish. Form tablespoons of dough into balls and drop into sugar, rolling gently to coat. Place on baking sheets, leaving 2 inches of space between. Press each lightly with your fingers into a rough disk.

5. Bake for 12 minutes. Let cookies cool for 2 to 3 minutes on pan, then transfer to rack. Store in an airtight container for up to 5 days.

Start With Brownies From a Boxed Mix...

Then, before you slice them, dress them up with irresistible toppings.

❶ MINTY GRASSHOPPER Beat 4 ounces softened cream cheese, 2 tablespoons unsalted butter and 1 cup confectioners' sugar in a stand mixer with the paddle attachment or with a hand mixer until smooth. Add 2 to 3 drops green food coloring and ½ teaspoon mint extract. Spread over cooled brownies.

❷ S'MORES-STYLE When brownies are almost done, top with 2 cups mini marshmallows and bake for 3 minutes or until marshmallows are browned.

❸ CARAMEL & PRETZEL Drizzle cooled brownies with ready-made caramel sauce (about ½ cup for a 9-inch square pan), then top with mini pretzels.

❹ CREAM CHEESE-SWIRLED Beat 4 ounces softened cream cheese with ¼ cup sugar, 1 tablespoon flour and 1 egg white. Pour over brownies before baking. Swirl with a knife and bake.

❺ PEANUT BUTTER & CHOCOLATE Microwave ½ cup creamy peanut butter for 30 seconds, then spoon into a zip-close plastic bag. Snip one corner of the bag with scissors and pipe softened peanut butter in stripes across surface of cooled brownies. Top with mini chocolate morsels.

Spiced Molasses Cookies

\|/
quick tip

Place each apple half between 2 chopsticks, skewers or dowels; they will prevent your knife from cutting all the way through the apple as you slice downward.

**Cinnamon
Hasselback Apples**

Cinnamon Hasselback Apples

Use a crisp, firm apple, such as Honeycrisp, that will hold its shape.

QUICK | SPECIAL OCCASION
TIME 40 minutes
(20 minutes active)
MAKES 6 servings

INGREDIENTS

Cooking spray
3 large Honeycrisp apples, peeled, halved vertically and cored
6 tablespoons dark brown sugar
4 tablespoons unsalted butter, melted
1½ teaspoons cinnamon
4 tablespoons old-fashioned rolled oats
2 teaspoons all-purpose flour
¼ teaspoon kosher salt

1. Preheat oven to 400 F. Coat a rectangular baking dish with cooking spray.
2. Place an apple half cut-side down on a cutting board. Starting near one end, cut each apple in ⅛-inch intervals, making sure not to cut all the way through. Repeat with remaining apple halves. Place apple halves, cut-side down, in baking dish. Cover baking dish with foil.
3. Bake for 10 minutes or until apples are tender. Remove from oven, uncover and let apples cool slightly.
4. In a small bowl, stir together remaining ingredients to make topping. With fingertips, carefully fan apple slices open slightly; spoon topping evenly over each. Bake, uncovered, 10 minutes more, then broil for 1 to 2 minutes to brown the topping. Serve with vanilla ice cream.

Chocolate Bourbon Balls

Chocolate Bourbon Balls

Put a boozy finish on the party with these no-bake treats.

EASY | SPECIAL OCCASION
TIME 40 minutes
(10 minutes active)
MAKES 48 servings

INGREDIENTS

3½ cups toasted pecans
1 (11-ounce) box vanilla wafers
½ cup heavy cream
¼ cup light corn syrup
8 ounces bittersweet chocolate chips
⅓ cup bourbon

1. In the bowl of a food processor, add pecans and pulse until finely chopped. Remove to a mixing bowl; reserve ½ cup for rolling. Place wafers in food processor and pulse until crumbled; add to nuts, stirring to mix.
2. In a microwave-safe liquid measuring cup, stir cream, corn syrup and chocolate chips; microwave in short bursts until melted, stirring each time. Let cool for 2 to 3 minutes, then whisk in bourbon. Pour melted chocolate mixture over wafer-nut mixture and stir to combine. Refrigerate for 30 minutes.
3. Spread reserved nuts in a wide, shallow dish. Line a baking sheet with parchment. Form tablespoons of chocolate mixture into balls and drop into nuts, rolling gently to coat; place on baking sheet as you finish. Store in an airtight container for up to 1 week.

Salted Caramel Pecan Sauce

Serve over vanilla ice cream or waffles—or just enjoy as is.

GLUTEN-FREE | SPECIAL OCCASION
TIME 30 minutes
(20 minutes active)
MAKES About 2½ cups

INGREDIENTS

- 1 cup sugar
- ½ cup water
- 1 cup heavy cream
- ½ teaspoon cinnamon
- ½ teaspoon sea salt
- ½ teaspoon vanilla extract
- ¼ cup unsalted butter, cubed
- ¾ cup chopped pecans, toasted

1. In a saucepan, stir together sugar and water. Heat over medium-high heat until mixture turns caramel-colored, about 15 to 20 minutes.
2. When time is almost up, in a microwave-safe liquid measuring cup, heat cream. On stove, reduce heat to low, whisk cream into sugar mixture and continue to cook 3 to 5 minutes, whisking constantly.
3. Whisk in cinnamon, salt, vanilla and butter. Stir in pecans. Serve sauce warm. Refrigerate in an airtight container for up to 5 days; microwave to rewarm.

Cinnamon-Apple Caramel Cheesecake Bars

You'll need to wait for the caramel to set before slicing into bars—but it'll be worth it!

EASY | FAMILY FAVORITE
TIME 3 hours
(30 minutes active)
MAKES 12 to 16 bars

INGREDIENTS

- Cooking spray
- 1 sleeve graham crackers
- 1 cup pecans
- 2 tablespoons unsalted butter, melted
- 1 pound cream cheese, at room temperature
- 2 eggs
- 1 (14-ounce) can sweetened condensed milk
- ¼ cup sour cream
- ¼ cup caramel sauce (such as Ghirardelli)
- ½ teaspoon kosher salt

FOR THE TOPPING

- 2 tablespoons unsalted butter
- ¼ cup dark brown sugar, packed
- 1 large apple, peeled and sliced thin
- ½ teaspoon cinnamon
- ¼ teaspoon nutmeg
- Pinch of clove
- Pinch of kosher salt
- ½ cup toasted pecans, finely chopped

1. Preheat oven to 350 F. Coat a 9-inch-square baking dish or 9-inch round springform pan with cooking spray.
2. In bowl of a food processor, add graham crackers and pulse to form fine crumbs. Add pecans and pulse until well chopped. Pour in melted butter and pulse until mixture resembles wet sand. Press mixture evenly into the bottom of prepared pan. Bake for 10 minutes; set aside.
3. In a stand mixer with a paddle attachment, or with a hand mixer, beat cream cheese until smooth, about 2 to 3 minutes. Beat in eggs, then condensed milk, sour cream, caramel and salt until smooth, about 3 to 5 minutes. Pour mixture over crust and bake 35 to 40 minutes or until center is set. Set aside to cool.
4. To make topping, in a large skillet over medium heat, melt butter. Stir in sugar, apples, spices and salt; cook 5 to 8 minutes, stirring occasionally, until apples are tender. Stir in pecans. Spoon apple mixture over caramel mixture. Refrigerate for 2 hours before cutting into bars.

Oat-Cranberry Lace Cookies

Be sure to watch these delicate cookies as they bake to prevent over-browning.

EASY | FAMILY FAVORITE
TIME 25 minutes
(10 minutes active)
MAKES 36 cookies

INGREDIENTS

- ½ cup butter
- 1 cup light brown sugar, packed
- ½ teaspoon kosher salt
- ½ teaspoon vanilla extract
- ¼ cup all-purpose flour
- 1½ teaspoons baking powder
- 1 egg, beaten
- 1 cup old-fashioned oats
- ¼ cup dried cranberries, chopped

1. Preheat oven to 325 F. Line 2 (or more) baking sheets with parchment.
2. In a medium microwave-safe bowl, add butter; microwave for 1 to 2 minutes to melt.
3. Whisk sugar, salt, vanilla, flour, baking powder and egg into butter. Stir in oats and cranberries.
4. Drop by teaspoonfuls onto parchment-lined baking sheets. leaving at least 2 to 3 inches between each (cookies will spread). You may need to work in batches. Bake 8 to 10 minutes or until golden brown. Cool pans on a rack until the cookies crisp up, about 1 hour.

Salted Caramel
Pecan Sauce

quick tip

Keep a close watch on
the caramel as it cooks;
the sugar mixture
can go quickly from
a just-right amber hue
to dark and burnt.

quick tip

Spray your hands as well as the baking dish with cooking spray. That way, the dough won't stick to them as you press it into the dish.

Cranberry-Maple Crumble Bars

Maple-Bourbon Pecan Pie

The pie offers a double dose of pecans—in the filling and the crust.

EASY | SPECIAL OCCASION
TIME 5 hours (20 minutes active)
MAKES 1 pie

INGREDIENTS

FOR THE CRUST

	Cooking spray
15	shortbread pecan cookies (such as Pecan Sandies)
¼	cup plus 2 tablespoons all-purpose flour
2	tablespoons unsalted butter

FOR THE FILLING

¼	cup plus 2 tablespoons unsalted butter
½	cup dark brown sugar
½	teaspoon kosher salt
¾	cup maple syrup
2	tablespoons bourbon
1	teaspoon vanilla extract
3	eggs
1½	cups toasted pecans

Maple-Bourbon Pecan Pie

1. Preheat oven to 350 F. Coat a 9-inch pie plate with cooking spray.

2. In a food processor, add the cookies and flour and pulse 5 or 6 times. Add butter and process until the mixture resembles wet sand. Press the mixture into the bottom and up the sides of the pie plate. Bake until lightly browned, 12 to 14 minutes. Cool completely on a rack, about 1 hour.

3. In a saucepan over medium heat, add butter, brown sugar and salt, stirring occasionally until melted, about 2 minutes. Whisk in syrup, bourbon and vanilla and reduce heat to medium-low.

4. In a large bowl, beat eggs. With a ladle, slowly pour ½ cup of butter mixture into beaten eggs, whisking constantly. Pour this egg mixture back into the sugar mixture and cook, stirring constantly, for 2 to 3 minutes more.

5. Stir in pecans and pour filling into prepared pie shell. Bake for 30 to 40 minutes or until center is set. Let cool on wire rack for 3 to 4 hours.

Cranberry-Maple Crumble Bars

Tangy cranberry contrasts with rich, buttery shortbread dough in these easy snack bars.

EASY | SPECIAL OCCASION
TIME 1 hour (15 minutes active)
MAKES 12 to 16 servings

INGREDIENTS

1	cup unsalted butter, at room temperature
¾	cup sugar
¼	teaspoon salt
½	teaspoon vanilla extract
2½	cups all-purpose flour
½	(14-ounce) can jellied cranberry sauce (about ¾ cup)
½	cup maple granola (such as Bear Naked)
¼	cup chopped walnuts
	Cooking spray
	Confectioners' sugar, for sprinkling

1. Preheat oven to 350 F. Coat a 9-inch square baking dish with cooking spray.

2. In a stand mixer with paddle attachment or using a hand mixer, cream butter, sugar and salt for 3 to 5 minutes. Stir in vanilla. Gradually add flour until dough forms, about 3 minutes.

3. Spoon ¾ of the dough into baking dish, using fingers to press it into the corners and ¼ inch up the sides. Spread cranberry sauce evenly on top of dough, leaving a ¼-inch border.

4. To remaining dough, mix in maple granola and walnuts using your hands; crumble on top of the cranberry mixture. Bake for 45 minutes. When cooled, sprinkle with the confectioners' sugar.

Recipe Index

CREDITS

Photography Jacqueline Stofsick   **Food Styling** Sarah Rideout
Additional Photography Volodymyr Kryshtal **7**; Goderuna **18**, **30**; kate_sun **66**;
Dorling Kindersley **78**; Sergio Bellotto **102**; Alhontess/Getty Images **110**

CENTENNIAL BOOKS

An Imprint of
Centennial Media, LLC
1111 Brickell Avenue, 10th Floor
Miami, FL 33131, U.S.A.

ISBN 978-1-951274-75-7

Distributed by
Simon & Schuster, Inc.
1230 Avenue of the Americas
New York, NY 10020, U.S.A.

For information about custom editions, special sales and premium and corporate purchases, please contact Centennial Media at contact@centennialmedia.com.

Manufactured in China

Publishers & Co-Founders Ben Harris, Sebastian Raatz
Editorial Director Annabel Vered
Creative Director Jessica Power
Executive Editor Janet Giovanelli
Design Director Martin Elfers
Features Editor Alyssa Shaffer
Deputy Editors Ron Kelly, Amy Miller Kravetz, Anne Marie O'Connor
Managing Editor Lisa Chambers
Senior Art Directors Lan Yin Bachelis, Pino Impastato
Art Directors Patrick Crowley, Alberto Diaz, Jaclyn Loney, Natali Suasnavas, Joseph Ulatowski
Copy/Production Patty Carroll, Angela Taormina
Senior Photo Editor Jenny Veiga
Production Manager Paul Rodina
Production Assistants Tiana Schippa, Alyssa Swiderski
Editorial Assistants Michael Foster, Alexis Rotnicki
Sales & Marketing Jeremy Nurnberg